# All Colour World of DOGS

# All Colour World of
# DOGS

David Squire

# Contents

Introduction 6

Choosing a puppy 8

Caring for your pet 19

A-Z of canine ailments 29

Family dogs 37

Breeding puppies 45

Toy breeds
and other small dogs 53

Sporting and
hunting breeds 62

Working with man 80

Obedience training 90

Dog shows 97

Index 104

Jacket: Golden Retriever
Endpapers: Basset Hound
Title page: Beagle puppies
This page: Saluki

First published 1978 by
Octopus Books Limited
59 Grosvenor Street
London W1

© 1978 Octopus Books Limited
ISBN 0 7094 0746 6

Produced by Mandarin Publishers Limited
22a Westlands Road
Quarry Bay, Hong Kong

Printed in Hong Kong

# Introduction

Dogs have achieved a unique place in our lives, often becoming a greatly treasured member of a household. They bring us immense joy and happiness; they cause a lot of anger and curses; they inspire in us love and affection, and they continually amaze us with their antics. They have earned themselves a place in our hearts, as well as by our hearths.

Dogs, like people, come in all shapes and sizes, and they display an equally wide spectrum of dispositions. Such differences between these creatures owe a lot to their forebears and the subsequent selective breeding of dogs by man.

If you wished to trace your dog's ancestry back to early times you might have a problem. From a zoological point of view the dog is not very ancient and was probably around about a million years ago. But there were carnivorous mammals millions of years before him. However, by the Neolithic Age the dog had been well and truly tamed and a real dog-and-man friendship was born.

The dog has achieved his status with man not because of his exceptional intelligence – cats can equal dogs in that respect – but because, unlike the cat, the dog is trainable and willing to help his owner.

The dog, of course, has some very wild relatives. That inoffensive and lovable creature nestling before your fire is scientifically a member of the *Canis* family, which includes the Wolf, Jackal, American Coyote and Australian Dingo.

Basically, the collective family term *Canis* suggests that these animals are structurally the same, with similar skull and teeth characteristics.

Throughout the world there are many wild dogs, with most of them in the New World and the majority in South America. In Asia reside the Buansuah and Raccoon-like Dog, while India, Sri Lanka (Ceylon), Malaya and Siberia each have their own species of wild dog. Africa is the home of the Somali Wild Dog and the African Wild Dog. North America has the Coyote, Gray Fox, Mexican Coyote and the Indian Territory Coyote. South America is extremely rich in wild dogs which include the Crab-eating Dog, Arecuna Hunting Dog, Colpeo, Santa Catharina Bush Dog and the Aguara-Guaza, often called the Maned Dog.

Whatever the dog's ancestry may have been it is true to say that the multiplicity of domestic breeds existing today ensures that all tastes and preferences can be satisfied. Each breed has its own characteristics which can be loved and enjoyed and have earned dogs their place as perhaps mankind's closest and most constant companion.

**Left: A well groomed and confident looking West Highland White Terrier surveys the world from his vantage point. Right: At the other end of the scale are these huge Irish Wolfhounds. They are tremendously powerful and are said to be the tallest members of the dog family.**

# Choosing a puppy

The question often posed: 'What breed of dog do you recommend?' is rather like asking your next door neighbour what motor car he advises you to buy. In both cases the choice is wide. And the answer to the question is that it all depends on what you want from the dog.

The range of breeds currently available is enormous, from the diminutive Chihuahua which weighs in at about 1 kg (2 lb) to an Irish Wolfhound at 54 kg (120 lb), and between them there is a vast range of shapes, sizes and colours to suit an equally wide range of tastes.

Family dogs are discussed in the chapter of that title, and a number of breeds are suggested as being safe with youngsters in the house.

In the chapters entitled 'Toy breeds', 'Sporting and hunting breeds' and 'Working with Man' many different breeds are described, but perhaps one of the best ways of selecting a dog is to go along to a local or national dog show and to see what different breeds look like and how they behave. Most owners are very willing to talk about the virtues and vices of their dogs, and this information can be invaluable to the prospective owner.

### Mongrel or Pedigree?

The question of whether to buy a pedigree or a mongrel dog is another evergreen question. Some people believe that a mongrel is more intelligent than a pedigree animal, and in certain cases this may be true. But the evidence tends to favour the pedigree dog. For instance, few mongrels work with the police, in the armed services or as civilian guard dogs, and dogs in these occupations have consistently to be intelligent and trainable. But mongrels should not be looked down upon unduly because they can make wonderful pets for the home.

The often recurring question of whether to have a bitch or a dog is discussed in 'Family dogs', and much of the decision depends on whether you have children

**Left:** The appeal and charm of puppies can be irresistible, but the responsibilities in keeping them must not be forgotten. It is all too easy to buy a young attractive puppy, but very sobering several months later to find you have a mature puppy needing daily attention and training.
**Right:** Growing puppies benefit from fresh air and sunshine. Basking in the warmth of a summer's day, these yellow Labrador puppies are quite content to while away their puppyhood.

in the house and are able to prevent a bitch from wandering when in season.

## Where to Find a Puppy

There are three main ways of obtaining a puppy: from a reputable dog breeder; from a local pet shop, or from a friend. And it is worth considering what each of these involves.

*Buying from a kennel.* The first decision to make is about the breed of dog you want, because if you are going to a kennel it is certain that you will be wanting a particular pedigree breed. Your local veterinary officer may be able to help with advice about a kennel specializing in the breed you want. If not, write to your national kennel club (enclosing a stamped and addressed envelope), asking for a list of kennels in your area with the breed of dog you want.

The next step is to visit the kennel and have a chat with the proprietor. It is doubtful if he would have a puppy that you could take away directly, as usually they are booked a long time in advance. But he will be able to advise you when puppies would be for sale.

Don't forget to discuss the price, as it is something both he and you need to be clear about. While at the kennel take the opportunity to check that it is clean and that the animals look healthy.

When buying from a kennel you can be reasonably sure that what the owner says about the dog is correct since his entire business rests upon his integrity. As an extra safeguard about the puppy's health, it is wise to have it checked by a qualified vet.

Some breeds produce their best puppies at certain times of the year, and it is worth consulting a person knowledgeable about the breed you are interested in to find out if this applies to your choice of dog.

*Buying from a pet shop.* The drawback with buying a dog from a pet shop is that it is usually impossible to check on the parents, their general health, breed, and so on. You will have to rely upon the word of the shop owner and use your own eyes to judge both the dog and the pet shop.

The shop should be tidy, with all of the animals looking clean and healthy. But it should not be so drenched in disinfectant that the smell might be hiding unpleasant aromas.

The dog, of course, may have passed through several other hands before it arrived at the shop, and it may even be the last of a litter and the puppy that nobody else wanted.

It is probable that the dog is a mongrel, and although this is nothing to worry about it is reassuring to have sight of the parents – or at least the mother. Again it is wise to have a veterinary officer check over the puppy before you buy him.

*Buying from a friend.* This can be one of the best ways to obtain a family dog, especially if you do not want a pedigree. The puppy will have been born in a house

and will have grown up in homely surroundings. This often makes it easier for the puppy to take to home life and people, especially children.

Try to have the pick of the litter, using the criteria suggested in the following section. Here again it is advisable to have a vet look over the animal to ensure that it is healthy.

## The Healthy Puppy

It is, of course, desirable to buy a healthy puppy. The points to look for, starting from the head, are a wet and cold nose, a pink and clean tongue, white teeth and bright and alert eyes.

The puppy's skin must be free from infection and disease. Check under his ears, especially if they are long, and under his leg joints.

He should be lively and should walk evenly on all of his legs, with no sign of weakness. Puppies which don't come forward to be stroked and fussed often do not make good pets. Young children – and especially daughters – tend to go for the smallest and most neglected puppies, which do not usually become more endearing with time and so, in the long term, they are a great disappointment to the whole family.

There is usually one puppy which stands out from his brothers and sisters by his general alertness and boldness. He may not be the largest, but he is certainly the puppy to have.

## Settling in the New Arrival

It is bound to be extremely frightening for a young puppy to leave his mother and suddenly to be put into a strange home. During this early period the new arrival will need understanding and attention to help him settle down happily.

Do take care at this stage, when the puppy is young, not to allow him to be plagued by children who might tire him. Many puppies are turned into bad tempered dogs by young people teasing them before they have learned to treat them properly.

When he arrives in his new home the puppy will be unaccustomed to lots of people bustling around, so for the first few days keep this to a minimum. He will enjoy, on the other hand, all the attention and admiration he is given. Friendly words of encouragement are what he will need initially, together with a warm and comfortable basket or box.

His box must be draughtproof and raised off the floor, where there might be very cold draughts. If possible, try to provide a box that he cannot get out of at night. This is for his own protection and safety, as small puppies can be very nosy and can easily get into difficult and dangerous situations. Also, in a busy kitchen in the morning, puppies do get under people's feet, much to their danger.

His first night in new surroundings will be his most difficult time, when he would normally be snuggling up to his mother for warmth, comfort and reassurance. Put a warm hot-water bottle securely wrapped in a small blanket in his box, against which he can nestle. He will also appreciate a soft cushion to rest on.

It will be necessary to show him his food and water bowls, which should not be too large as he may find it very difficult to eat and drink from them or he may even fall into them.

During these early days of settling in it is all too easy to be cruelly kind to the pup and pick him up at

**Left:** This attractive and lively little Jack Russell Terrier can be a mischievous imp, full of high spirits and intelligence. **Below:** Cats and dogs are not always antagonistic towards each other, as many households with both kinds of pet can testify.

night and take him to bed with you. This initially makes the puppy very comfortable, but it is far better to make the puppy comfortable in his box or basket and to make him clearly understand where his sleeping place is.

**Housetraining the Puppy**
The objective of housetraining is quite clear, and that is to make the puppy attend to his natural functions outside in the garden and not to relieve himself on the carpet in front of the fire. To do this makes sense as far as the puppy is concerned, for it saves him a walk, often on a cold winter's night. But for reasons of hygiene it is important to break the puppy of this habit as soon as he has settled in.

Fortunately it is not difficult to housetrain puppies, and they are usually quick and eager to learn. No puppy will want to spoil his bed and therefore he will be pleased to go outside.

The technique of training him revolves around using the voice both to reward him and to scold him. Don't resort to smacks as you will frighten him. This will easily be understood by looking at the situation from the animal's point of view. If a puppy has always used the floor as a lavatory, suddenly to be hit for doing what you have always done is disturbing, if not frightening, and will make the puppy lose all confidence in his new master. Rather, reward the puppy with a smile and a happy voice with a 'Good boy', or with a scowl and 'Bad boy'.

The daily housetraining routine begins early in the morning, as soon as you get up. Put the puppy outside in the garden. But don't leave him in the garden on his own; stay with him until he has performed, when he should be rewarded with the words 'Good boy' and a smile.

To emphasize where he is going, say 'Garden' as you take him out. Keep the number of different words to the minimum, such as 'Good boy', 'Bad boy' and 'Garden' and use your voice to indicate pleasure or displeasure.

Repeat this process every few hours, especially after meals. If he does have an accident, don't let your own irritation take charge and smack him, just say 'Bad boy' and take him outside, saying 'Garden'. By this method a puppy will become housetrained within a very short time.

Below: This Dalmatian puppy is delighting in playing with a piece of sacking attached to a string. Right: This German Shepherd Dog puppy will grow into a powerful dog requiring firm control. They make excellent guard dogs.

**A Time to Go**
It may be as well, at this point, to give some thought to the end of your pet's life because parting with a dog you have known from puppyhood is something which comes to all pet owners.

The life span of the dog much depends on the breed, but on average you can expect your pet to be with you from nine to fourteen years, perhaps even more. Remember that from the age of eight or nine he will begin to lose his sharpness. At this stage he is entering old age and will need more attention from you. Happily, as with humans, dogs now live longer than they did in the 1940s and 1950s, and this is the result of better foods and veterinary care. Also, a pleasant home life and abundant affection will keep the dog happy and contented.

There comes a time, however, when a dog, although being loved and cared for with the greatest attention and affection, reaches a stage when it would be selfish to keep him alive. And it is at this time that great courage is required. Ask a vet's opinion about his health and if the recommendation is to have him put down, do take his advice. To keep an ailing dog is cruel and selfish.

Take your dog to the vet or call him round, and while you distract the dog's attention he will give a painless injection that will put your treasured friend to sleep.

**Previous pages:** The degree of alertness, curiosity and boldness shown by puppies is a good guide to their future development.

**Below:** Cocker Spaniels are very popular, although their coats do require a lot of attention. **Right:** Fox Terriers are hardy dogs. They are often run with hounds and used to chase out foxes which have gone to earth.

# Caring for your pet

Owning a dog brings many pleasures and moments of pride, but it also carries responsibilities which cannot be neglected if your pet is to remain in good health.

Dogs like a routine which they know and understand. This should include meals at certain times, regular exercise, frequent brushing and grooming and even knowing where they are to sit during a motor car journey.

Puppies and dogs are keen to learn and to please their owners, who can make their own and their dogs' lives happy, by treating them with understanding tempered with firmness.

**Feeding the Puppy**
One of the most important considerations with a puppy is to give him the correct amount of the right food at a set time. A week or so before collecting your puppy, therefore, have a word with the breeder from whom you are buying him and ask what his current diet is, how many meals a day he has, and so on.

It is probable that the pup will be somewhere around ten to twelve weeks old, and already weaned from his mother's milk on to solid and semi-solid foods. But at this stage his stomach is very small and it must not be overloaded with food. Puppies who have gorged themselves will have distended stomachs which in turn tend to put a severe strain on their backs and legs. Furthermore, a puppy which has been overfed and become fat may go off his food later in life.

What a puppy needs for bone and flesh development is a diet rich in proteins, such as fish, eggs, milk and meat. These foods also help to ward off infections and minimize the possibility of ill-health.

Young puppies need regular meals. At about ten weeks old five a day is about right. The amount at each meal should be no more than the pup will hungrily eat up. If the pup has to labour over his food, with frequent and long pauses while eating then the meal is too large.

Spread the meals over fifteen to sixteen hours, at about four-hour intervals. At breakfast, a cereal and fine biscuit mixed in warm milk, into which has been

**Left:** Greyhounds are a very ancient breed, which used to hunt by sight. Nowadays they are highly prized competitors at racetracks. **Below:** When puppies feed at the same dish the weaker and less determined may be kept back. Separate dishes would ensure that they all get a fair share.

The Rough-coated Collie is one of the most attractive and intelligent of dogs, often used to herd sheep.

beaten an egg, will be very nourishing. Also mix in a dessertspoon of rusks which contains several vitamins and other essential elements.

At lunchtime, lightly cooked mince, or liver, fish or tripe, moistened with gravy is advised. In the afternoon, a drink of warm milk should be given. Then, in the early evening repeat his midday meal, and at bedtime repeat his breakfast, plus a few biscuits.

It is essential that meals, other than those chiefly formed of milk, should not be swimming in moisture. Indeed, as the pup gets older his food should become drier.

Some people advocate raw meat, others that it should be slightly cooked. Much depends on the puppy's preference. If the meat is quite fresh it can be fed to the puppy raw, but in some cases a pup will not be able to digest uncooked meat; he may have an aversion to it.

During this time it is essential that the pup should have a bowl of fresh drinking water. Indeed, this must continue throughout his life.

By the time he reaches fifteen weeks he will probably start to refuse the milk, especially at bedtime. But do ensure he continues with his bedtime biscuits.

At four months the number of feeds can be reduced to four and at six months to two feeds a day. It is at this stage that he can go on to his adult diet.

**Feeding the Adult Animal**
Adult dogs eventually require only one good meal a day, plus a bedtime snack. But the transitional stage from two meals to one meal will depend on the breed of dog you have. For instance, a large dog takes much longer to reach maturity than a small one. Very large dogs often take up to eighteen months or even two years, during which time their bodies are developing

Far left: The Lhasa Apso is a breed from Tibet that needs plenty of grooming, and is known to have existed for over 800 years. He is extremely hardy and watchful and very responsive to love and kindness. Left: The Bearded Collie is a distinctive breed which at one time was on the decline. Happily he is now known as a superb family dog. When grooming, sit him on a table or box – it makes brushing more easy.

in height and size. Small dogs usually mature between eight and ten months, at which time they can be put on one meal a day, plus a bedtime snack of biscuits.

It is essential that the quality of the meals is high and that the dogs are not fed only on non-nutritious scraps of food nobody else wants, such as cold potatoes and scraps of stale bread. If you want a healthy dog, then the meals must be well balanced, containing the right proportions of proteins and carbohydrates.

Proteins are muscle-forming foods, building a strong bone structure and feeding the nerves, brain, coat and skin. They are contained in foods such as meat, liver and herrings, and, in the food consumed by domestic animals, they are normally of animal origin.

Your dog also needs carbohydrates as an essential part of his diet. In practice, carbohydrates do form a major part in bulk of the dog's diet, usually around 60 per cent. If there is more, essential proteins may be crowded out of his diet.

Carbohydrates are to be found in sugar and starch foods, such as potatoes, cane sugar, milk and rice. Foods with a high starch content must be cooked, as uncooked starch foods are very difficult to digest. If your dog likes starchy foods and does not show any signs of becoming fat, then let him have them in moderation.

The question often arises as to when it is best to give your dog his main meal. This is usually either a midday meal or an evening meal, but whichever you choose it is essential to adopt a routine, so the dog knows when to expect his main meal.

Many experts advocate a meal in the early evening, as the dog can then doze off quite happily because he is not expected to be so lively at that time as he would in the afternoon after a midday meal.

At bedtime, give him a snack of biscuits. This is something he will look forward to.

By the way, if your dog has long ears, which would normally trail in the food, stand his bowl on a slightly raised box.

## Grooming

Few things are worse in the home than a ragged coated, smelly dog. He is a misery to himself and an eyesore to those who live with him. But when he is kept clean with daily brushings and groomings he becomes a new dog and a pleasure to have around the house. And healthy, well groomed dogs are always to be admired.

A young puppy needs little grooming, but it is advisable from an early stage to get him used to his daily inspection and brushing. Let him think it is playtime at first, so that he takes an interest in it. Then gradually train him to stand still during this grooming period.

*Brushing.* This is best achieved by standing the dog on a platform or box, so enabling a complete and detailed

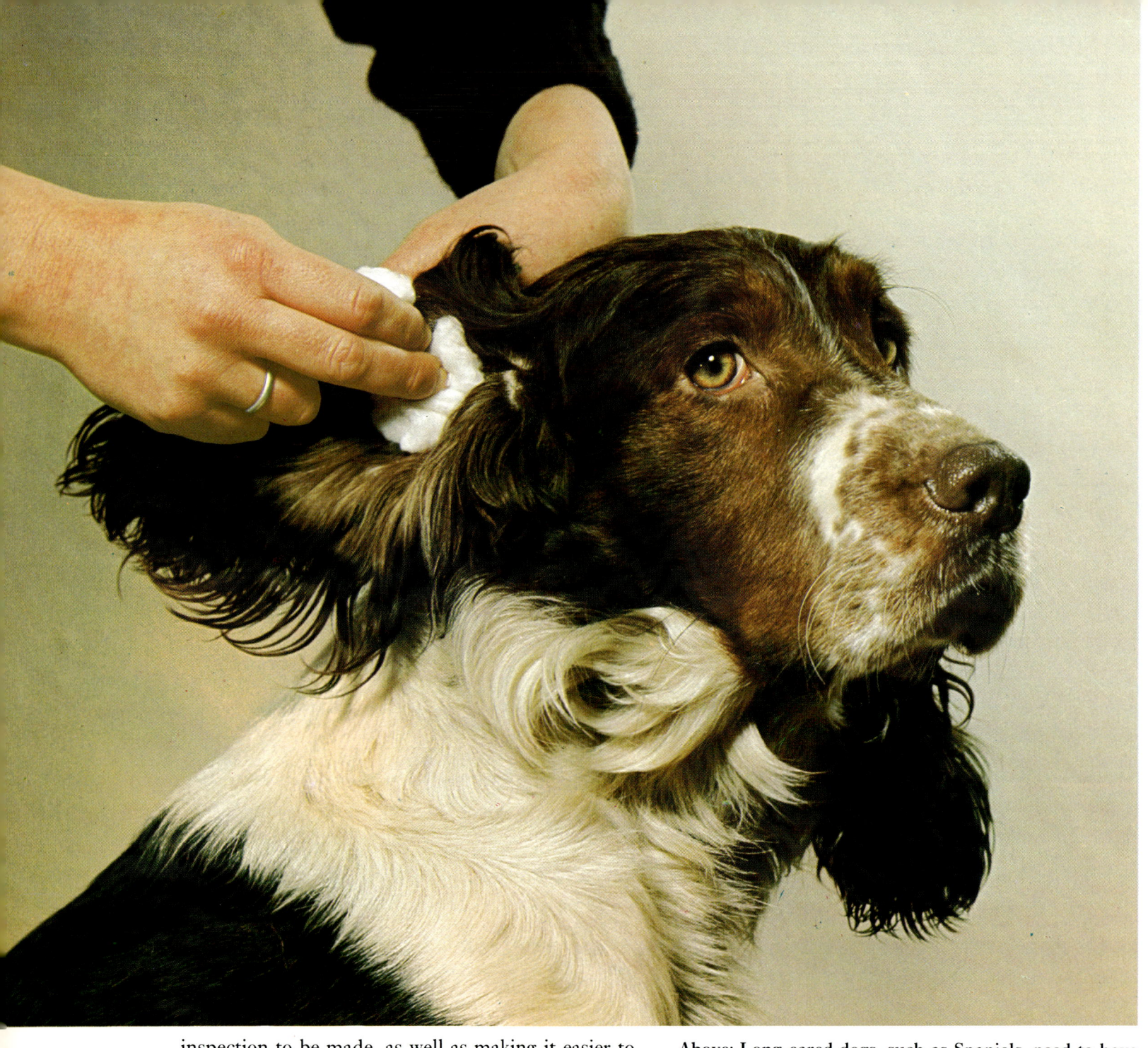

inspection to be made, as well as making it easier to work on him. The amount of time spent each day on brushing will, of course, depend on the breed of dog. Smooth coated types, such as a Dachshund or smooth terrier, may require only a few minutes. On the other hand, an Old English Sheepdog may need fifteen to thirty minutes.

Long-haired dogs and especially those with curly coats must be kept well groomed, as otherwise the coat becomes such a tangle that it can be painful to the dog and difficult to bring back into good condition.

Brushing, of course, not only makes the dog look pleasant and more presentable, but removes dust, dirt and scurf from the coat and stimulates the skin and muscles, keeping them supple and encouraging healthy hair to grow.

If you have a dog with a smooth coat, you'll need a short-bristled brush, a hound glove and a soft cloth.

Above: Long-eared dogs, such as Spaniels, need to have their ears kept clean. It is best to use cotton wool wrung out in water with a little surgical spirit added.

The first job is to use the brush briskly to free the coat of dandruff and dust. Then, go over all parts of the head, body and limbs with the hound glove. Finish off with the soft cloth to give the coat a shine.

For a long haired coat a coarse toothed comb is needed and a brush with bristles long enough to penetrate through the hair right to the skin. When grooming a long haired dog it often becomes necessary to lift up the coat and brush a small patch at a time.

With wire haired dogs, the comb needs to be smaller and the teeth closer together. You will also need a stiff brush. Use the comb to remove all loose hairs, then brush the coat, taking the bristles down to the base of the hairs.

*Trimming.* Certain types of dog will require

professional trimming several times a year to keep them looking smart and neat. Such breeds as trimmed terriers – Welsh, Airedale, and Lakeland Terriers, Wire-haired Fox Terriers – require this treatment. If left untrimmed, the coats of these dogs become thick and ragged, completely hiding the animal's shape.

*Clipping.* This is chiefly required by poodles, and the pattern to which the coat is clipped is usually left to the discretion of the owner. Indeed, there is no need to clip a large poodle at all if you like a more natural appearance.

*Bathing.* Well groomed dogs seldom need a bath. Indeed, washing the dog tends to remove the protective and natural oils from the coat and skin. But if you have to, and this often comes about because the animal has rolled in something unpleasant, use warm water and a medicated shampoo. Don't make do with household soap or detergents which cause skin disorders.

Wash and soak him thoroughly, with several rinses to ensure all the soap is removed. Start at the shoulders of the animal and work downwards, taking special care with the feet to remove all mud and dirt. Finish off by using a moist sponge on his face, taking care not to get any water in eyes or ears. Dry the animal thoroughly, wiping inside the ears with a soft cloth to ensure that they are dry.

A normal dog's inclination after being bathed is directly to roll in some more dirt, so keep an eye on him!

*Cleaning ears.* Daily attention to your dog's ears is most important. This is especially so if he has long ears. In the next chapter, canker of the ear is described, and this is very debilitating and irritating to the animal. Prevention is very important, and this entails wiping the inside of the ear flaps with methylated or surgical spirit, drying them thoroughly afterwards.

## Exercising the Animal

Regular daily exercise is absolutely essential for good health in your dog. The amount required will, of course, depend on the breed. Beagles and Boxers, for instance, will require more than an hour, while a toy only thirty minutes.

Regular exercise and basic lead training should be started when the dog is a puppy. And the first step is to accustom the pup to wearing a collar. This is best done during play and to allow him to continue playing afterwards, so distracting his attention from something new around his neck. All collars should be removed at night.

As soon as he is used to a collar, a light cord can be attached to it. Allow the lead to trail, so that the pup realizes it is part of the collar and not something to be afraid of. This all takes time, but it is essential for the puppy to accept it and not to be frightened of it.

When he is accustomed to the collar and lead, gently lift up the lead and let him know he can be guided. Do this quite gently at first, so that he is not alarmed.

All of this is necessary to get him used to some form of training, but real road exercises cannot be given until he is a little more mature, at about six months or more. He will then be steadier in temperament and easier to control.

## Travelling With Your Dog

It is always surprising how well dogs take to motor car travel. Most puppies, however, are car sick at first. This is quite understandable, especially if they are not slowly introduced to car travel. They will probably experience a sense of claustrophobia and a lack of fresh air.

The answer to this problem is to take him on very short trips first of all, such as to the local shop or to get the newspaper. He will probably vomit at first, so take care that the car seat is protected by a sheet or towel, and remember he has no respect for your best suit, so dress accordingly or cover yourself.

If he is still sick after a long period of short trips, consult your vet. A sure sign that he is going to vomit is when he starts to swallow a great deal and licks his lips in an excited manner. Stop the car and allow him to breathe fresh air. But as with most pups he will soon grow to like car travel, insisting that he goes on every journey.

In summer cars can get hot extremely quickly and if your dog is left inside he may well suffer heat stroke. To minimize the risk of this happening, slightly lower one or, preferably, two windows and park the car in the shade.

## Boarding Kennels

Most owners at some time or other have to put their dog into a boarding kennel. If you do not know of a good kennel it would be best to have a word with your local veterinary officer who will advise you. This should also ensure that your dog does not have a traumatic stay in a badly run kennel.

Before putting your dog into their care, and to reassure yourself, go along and inspect the kennel. Look for a clean and sweet-smelling place, not littered with uneaten food and dog droppings. Drinking dishes, bowls and other utensils should also be clean.

If your dog has a special diet or needs certain medical treatment, do discuss this with the kennel owner. And as a safeguard leave an address at which you can be reached in an emergency.

## Car Chasing

Your dog may have sporting inclinations and take up chasing motorcars, motorcyclists and bicyclists. This should be frowned upon and steps taken to stop such activity. The best way of prevention, of course, is to keep the dog on a leash when in the street, but it may not at first be possible to stop him running out of your garden and pursuing a car.

This dangerous habit usually starts in a small way and the dog, if uncorrected, can go on to take it up as a full time occupation. If normal training does not stop him, extraordinary treatment is required. Tie a twenty foot rope to the dog, not simply around his neck but attaching it to the animal by a harness, and holding the other end firmly. When the dog next runs after a car he will be suddenly pulled up as soon as he has run the distance and the shock will probably pull him off his feet.

### Barking, Howling and Baying

Nothing is worse than living next door to a dog given to barking or howling. If your dog barks incessantly, then expect your neighbours to protest about it.

There are, of course, breeds which are by nature noisy. For instance, the Belgian Barge Dog is a yappy dog, determined to protect his owner's property. If you have a hound, then he may bay. But it is the extent to which he does this that is important. For a dog to bark when the door bell is rung or when the telephone rings and then keep quiet is quite acceptable.

Puppies can be trained not to bark continuously. As soon as the bell goes and the puppy barks allow him two or three barks, then say 'No' to him. He will eventually get the message.

With mature dogs the problem is increased. However, don't just let him bark, show him that he has met with your displeasure.

One cause of continual barking and howling is if the dog is highly strung and is left on his own for long periods. He does not know what to do and so to amuse himself he exercises his voice and lungs. The answer is either not to leave the dog alone or not have a dog.

If at the end of all coercion the dog still barks, have a word with your veterinary officer as he may be able to suggest some treatment.

### Biting

Some dogs bite adults and children, and perhaps on very rare occasions there might be a legitimate reason for this. Nevertheless, countries have laws against this trait and it must always be discouraged.

Most owners of snappy dogs know of their dog's propensity to bite and so they take due care, but danger can arise when people visit a house not knowing of a dog's tendency to bite.

There are numerous reasons why a dog will bite people. He may be a snappy breed which by instinct is protective of property or has a herding instinct. Dogs pestered by children may bite. Old age brings a lack of tolerance in the animal, especially if he is ill. Nervous and highly strung dogs will also bite, often for no reason.

For safety's sake, it is best to make sure that all of your family and visitors know of the problem and try to prevent strangers from coming into contact with the animal.

**Left:** The Borzoi, like the Deerhound, was bred for speed. His other name is the Russian Wolfhound and at one time they were used by Russian tsars to hunt wolves. Their coats are long and silky and can be any colour. **Right:** Small dogs often appreciate shelter from strong sun during the summer.

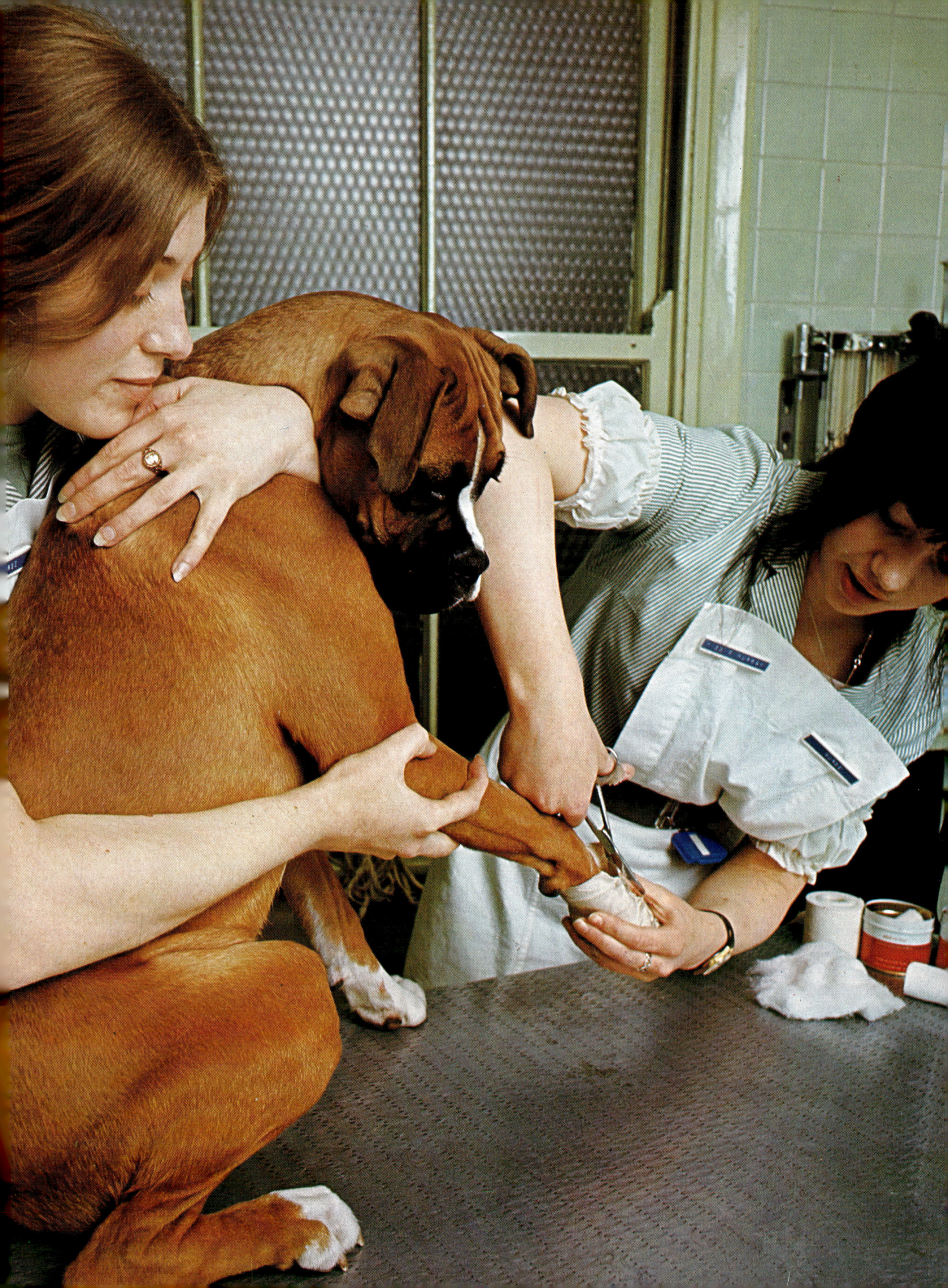

# A-Z of canine ailments

All pets, at some time in their lives, fall ill and require medical treatment either of a first-aid nature in the home or from a qualified veterinary officer.

Looking after animals, in sickness as well as when in good health, is a responsibility not to be shirked by any dog owner. Dogs give a great deal of pleasure to their owners and it is only right that a caring attitude to them should be adopted when they are ill.

Perhaps the golden rule, when the dog is unwell, is not to guess at the cause of the trouble. It is best to take him along to a vet, or in an emergency ask the vet to call. And don't try any of those 'quack' remedies that someone's great aunt may suggest, nor should you use up ointment or lotion left over from a family illness. Ointments can lose their healing properties after only a few months, and in any case it is specialized treatment that your pet requires.

Many of the ailments and problems your dog may encounter are listed in this chapter, but I do emphasize that expert veterinary attention may be required. Many illnesses, when caught in their early stages, do not become problems, but if they are left hopefully to cure themselves or if they are not treated professionally, then it is possible that your treasured pet may suffer unnecessarily and may even die.

*Abscesses.* These are inflamed and painful swellings containing pus, accompanied by localized pain and a rise in temperature. The swelling, however, is caused

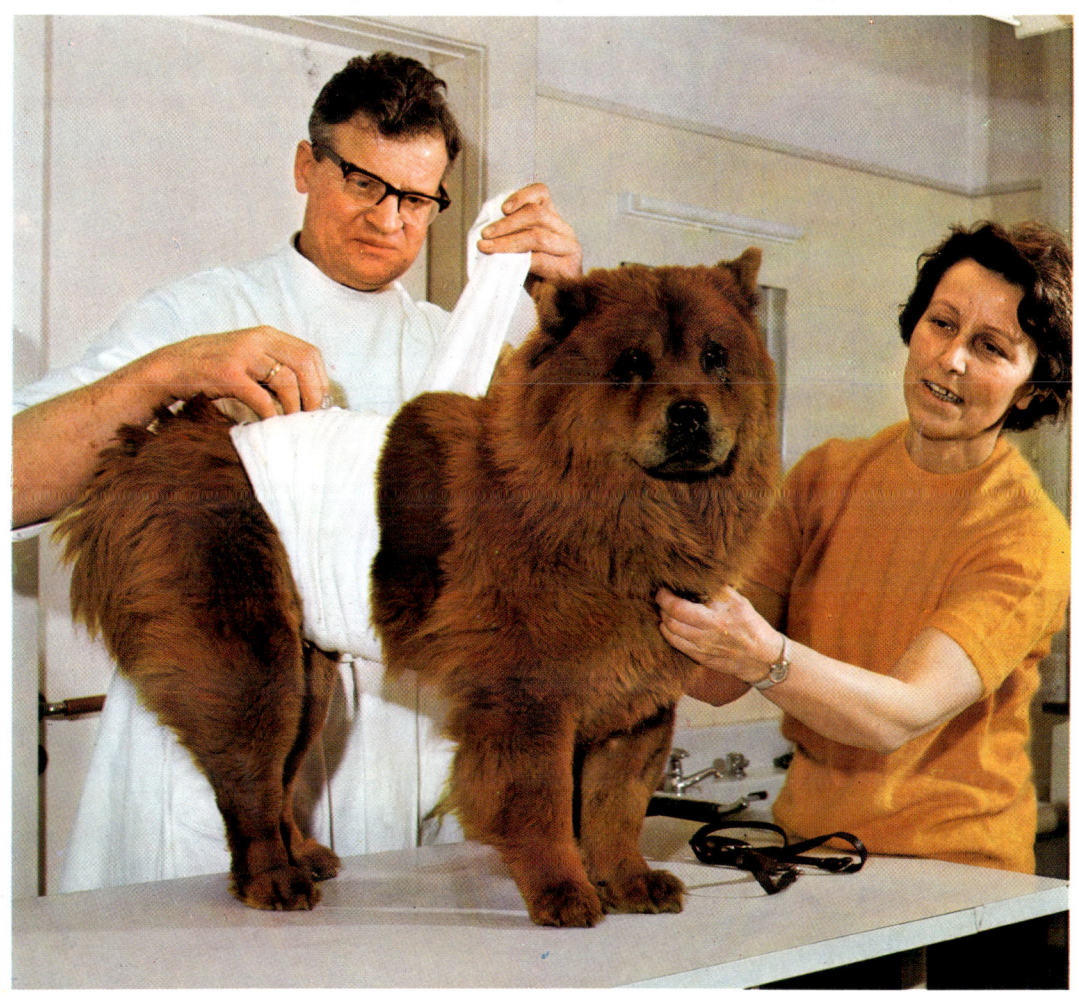

Left: A visit to a veterinary officer need not be an ordeal for a dog if he learns he is being helped and is among friends. This Boxer is gently held and comforted while his injured paw receives attention. Right: A vet dressing a wound after treatment. The Chow Chow's owner is comforting and reassuring her dog.

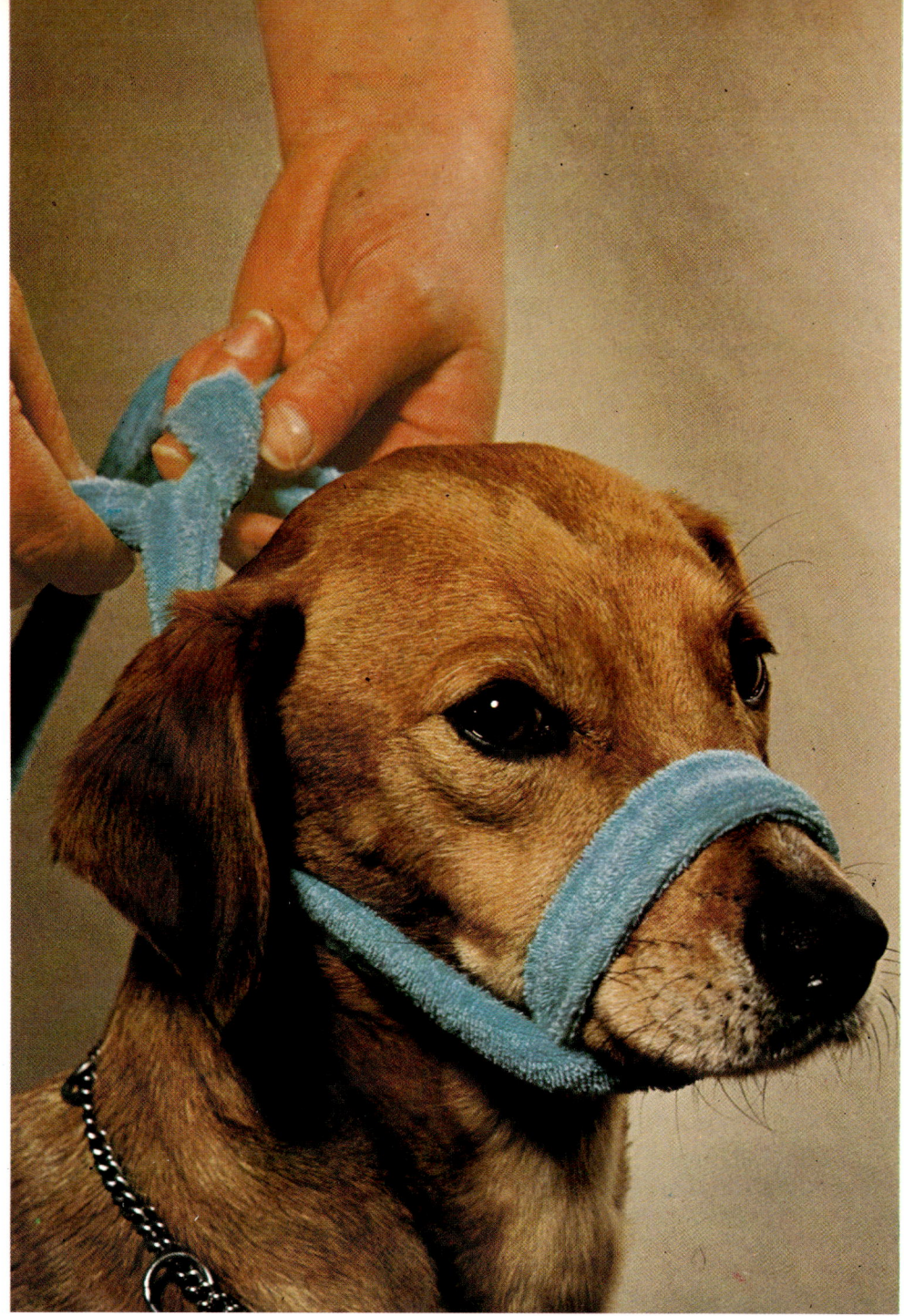

Left: Occasionally it is necessary to muzzle a dog before treatment. At such times a length of bandage or soft towelling can be used, winding it around the jaws and tying at the back of the neck. Do ensure that the dog's breathing is not restricted by the muzzle. Right: A dog's temperature can be taken by holding him firmly and inserting a blunt-nosed thermometer into his rectum and leaving it there for three minutes. A dog's normal temperature is 38°C (101.5°F).

by a local infection. Do not squeeze the abscess, but allow it to burst naturally.

There are two main methods of encouraging the abscess to burst: by bathing the area in a warm salt-water solution, or by covering the abscess with hot compresses until it bursts. When this happens wash with a solution of Milton, Savlon or TCP.

It is essential to drain the abscess thoroughly, so bathe the area every three hours for a couple of days after it bursts.

*Arthritis.* This is an ailment from which an old dog often suffers, and the best way to help is to keep him warm and dry. His joints become stiff, he will have trouble in walking, and will become snappy and irritable. Have a word with your vet.

*Bandaging.* There are five main uses for bandages: to stop bleeding; to prevent the animal from nibbling and biting its injuries; to reduce and relieve swelling; to support injured limbs, and to prevent an open wound from being infected. In practice, it is usually only in emergencies that a bandage is needed. The only other time is when the animal has been ill and is being treated by the vet. In that case, the vet will show how the bandage is applied.

Occasionally a strong bandage can be used as a muzzle – this is useful when treating a snappy dog. But take care not to restrict the dog's breathing.

*Bites.* There are two main types of bite received by dogs, and both are usually the result of fights. These are punctures and lacerations. If slight, clean them with an antiseptic diluted in warm water. But if the skin is deeply and badly torn – or if bits of the animal are missing – take the dog to a vet.

*Bladder infection.* Dogs are prone to bladder infections, the symptoms of which are varied. They include abdominal pain, loss of appetite, straining to pass urine, frequent urination and traces of blood in the urine. Consult your vet as soon as possible.

*Broken bones.* If your dog suffers a fracture of any kind. Do not attempt home treatment but keep him warm and consult a vet rapidly.

*Broken teeth.* Occasionally your dog may tackle something much harder than his teeth and, as a result he may break a tooth. Fortunately, this does not hurt the dog, but it may cause bad breath, dribbling or bleeding from the gums. Eventually the tooth may have to be extracted.

*Bronchitis.* This will cause excessive coughing, often accompanied by phlegm. To ensure that it is bronchitis, check that the cough is not caused by a foreign body in the throat.

Bronchitis can be treated with codeine linctus. Do not give the dog any food for at least 24 hours, then only a small amount. Consult a vet if the dog is still coughing after 48 hours.

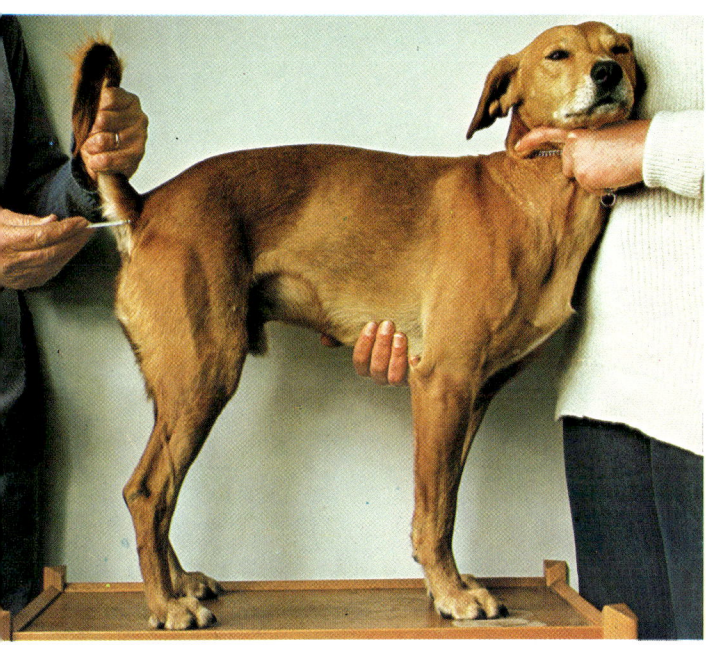

*Burns and scalds.* These most commonly occur in the home. Scalds are due to contact with moist heat, whereas burns result from dry heat. In practice, the treatment is the same.

Dogs badly burnt tend to be snappy, so you may have to resort to a cloth muzzle when treating him. The dog may be in shock, so keep him warm and give a drink of warm water and glucose. Severely burned dogs must be taken to a vet, as secondary infection may occur. Light burns may be cleaned and an antiseptic ointment applied to the area.

*Canker.* This is an extremely painful condition, caused by tiny parasites in the canal of the ear. It causes extreme irritation. It sometimes attacks the inside of the ear-flaps, causing sores to appear.

The treatment of an infection in an advanced stage calls for the services of a vet. Probing into a dog's ear is highly specialized and should always be left to a vet. In the early stages treatment with insecticidal ear drops will clear the condition.

*Canine hepatitis.* This is a highly contagious virus which attacks dogs, often fatally. It is often called Rubarth's Disease.

It is usually encountered in one of three degrees. First, if a dog contracts it in an acute way, death inevitably results. Total collapse may occur within only a few hours of a normal and healthy condition.

The second way is the more common, in that the dog displays mild signs of being ill. The animal may be lethargic and have swollen and inflamed tonsils. Puppies will just sit in their sleeping box, instead of romping about the house.

The third way is when a dog has the disease, but shows no sign of being infected. In this state the dog transmits the virus through urine and excreta to other dogs.

The golden rule when you are faced with this disease is to get veterinary advice rapidly. Also, have puppies inoculated against the virus as soon as they are eight weeks old. And, as an added precaution, do not let puppies near other dogs until they have been inoculated.

*Choking.* This occurs when either a foreign body or the tongue is blocking the throat, preventing breathing. Treatment is needed rapidly. Open the dog's mouth and if the tongue is curled back blocking the throat, hook your finger around it and pull it forward. If the blockage is due to a foreign body, try to hook it out – do not push it down the throat. If the object is firmly lodged, trickle a little olive oil down the throat.

*Constipation.* From time to time dogs become constipated. The dog can be seen straining, passing a watery discharge, bleeding and perhaps vomiting. Starve the dog and give him 45–75 ml (3–5 tablespoons) of liquid paraffin. If he has not recovered within 36 hours, consult your vet.

*Diarrhoea.* Dogs often suffer mild attacks of diarrhoea, which may be accompanied by vomiting. Water and food should be withheld for a day or so, and then only a limited amount should be given for a further three or four days. Often, by this time, the diarrhoea will have subsided but severe attacks can be treated by administering codeine phosphate. If diarrhoea persists for three to four days consult your vet.

*Distemper.* This is a highly infectious virus that can infect dogs of all ages – those suspected of having contracted it should be isolated. The incubation period can be anything from three to fifteen days. Prevention is best and immunity can be provided by annual vaccinations. Your vet can advise you about this.

The symptoms in infected dogs are listlessness, a high temperature (about 40°C (105°F)), lack of appetite, dry cough, discharge from the eyes and, eventually, vomiting and diarrhoea. A subsequent stage may be convulsions and twitching of muscles on the dog's forelegs and face. Seek your vet's advice as soon as possible.

Your dog's temperature can be taken by holding him firmly and gently inserting a blunt-nosed thermometer into his rectum, leaving it there for three minutes. Don't forget first to smear the thermometer with Vaseline or soap. The temperature of a healthy dog is 38°C (101.5°F). If the temperature is above or below this figure, consult a vet.

*Ear troubles.* Dogs are susceptible to ears being torn during fights, and they can bleed alarmingly. Clean them up with Cetavlon.

The other troublesome ear problem is canker, and to combat this see under that entry. Always check the ears regularly and keep the ear flaps clean.

*Eczema.* This is inflammation of the skin. It is not contagious and is mainly caused through blood disorders. The dog becomes irritated and bites and scratches his skin, making it red and sore. The hair, by this time, has been rubbed away and there appears a bare area, anything from 25–150 mm (1–6 in) across.

Apply a solution of a few potassium permanganate crystals in 275 ml ($\frac{1}{2}$ pt) of water to the area. Then wash the entire dog thoroughly and dab calamine lotion on the bare areas.

*Eye troubles.* With any eye problem, get professional help. In an emergency, wrap a soft bandage or cloth around the head and eye.

*Fits.* These can take several forms, all of which are highly frightening to the owner and the dog. In practice, there is very little to be done for the dog, other than preventing him from hurting himself or attacking and biting anyone. If possible, try to direct him into a room with blankets on the floor. Call a vet.

Left: A Labrador mother snoozes beside her puppies, although at this stage the bitch often likes to get a little peace by sleeping away from the litter. A floor covering of newspaper is the most economical for puppies reared indoors as it can be changed at frequent intervals. When the puppies are about four weeks old they will probably try to climb out of their box and explore the world. Right: Dogs which have been injured in an accident need gentle treatment. Use a blanket or sheet to lift the dog to take him to a veterinary officer.

*Fleas.* It is probable that at some time in your dog's life he will encounter fleas. They cause intense irritation and annoyance to the dog, as well as transmitting the eggs of tapeworms. Don't worry if your dog's fleas bite you – it's only a passing fancy as they cannot live on humans.

To check if the dog has fleas, part the hair. If small, reddish and flat creatures are noticed – or if tiny particles of black grit, which are flea droppings, are seen – the dog has fleas.

Ridding the dog of its unwelcome lodgers involves warm baths every other day for two weeks. At the same time, ensure that his bedding is clean, dusting it with pyrethrum powder or derris powder. On the days when the dog is not being bathed, dust him with pyrethrum powder.

If your puppy has fleas and is under eight weeks, do not powder him. Instead, bath him in a diluted selenium shampoo, ensuring it is well rinsed off.

*Gastritis.* This is an inflammation of the stomach, usually resulting from over-eating, eating contaminated food or the presence of indigestible food in the stomach. The symptoms are violent and frequent vomiting, marked thirst and diarrhoea. The treatment is to keep the dog warm, and all food and water should be withheld for 24 hours. Then feed him bland foods such as broth, soft eggs and milk. If the trouble persists, seek the advice of a vet.

*Hard pad.* This is a variety of distemper. All the basic symptoms are the same, with the addition of severe diarrhoea and hardening of the foot pads and nose. It is essential to consult a vet as quickly as possible.

*Heat stroke.* This is obviously due to over exposure to the sun or heat. The usual cause is when a dog has been shut up in a car without sufficient ventilation. The symptoms are excessive panting, dullness and sweating through foot pads. Give the dog water straightaway and try to cool him by spraying with water. Ice packs to the head and chest help.

*Hysteria.* The dog suddenly shows intense fear and excitement without any apparent reason. Hysteria can be distinguished from a fit as the animal does not collapse or froth at the mouth. He may run wildly about the room, barking and bouncing off walls and furniture. Treatment is as for fits.

*Indigestion.* This becomes apparent chiefly when the dog vomits and is especially prevalent in young animals. It is usually due either to the dog eating too much food, eating far too fast, excessive activity directly after eating or through eating a non-food substance, such as newspaper, chair stuffing, cigarette ends, and so on.

Treatment for slight indigestion is Milk of Magnesia, but if the trouble reoccurs quickly or does not subside, consult a vet.

*Leptospirosis.* Take care with this bacterial disease, as it is highly contagious and easily transmitted to humans. It is passed from dog to dog by infected urine. Puppies and male dogs are more frequent sufferers than bitches.

Infected dogs become lethargic, thirsty, disinterested in food and have a sore stomach. Subsequently, the dog moves in pain and has a high temperature, up to 41°C (106°F), accompanied by vomiting and diarrhoea.

The only treatment is to get professional help. And

take care that your family wash their hands thoroughly after touching the dog. Consult your vet and have the dog vaccinated annually.

*Lice.* These are flat little creatures which crawl slowly through and around the base of the dog's hair. They are easily distinguished from fleas, which tend to run and jump through the dog's coat.

Treatment is quite easy. Just bath and shampoo the dog every week for up to four weeks using an insecticidal shampoo, such as one containing selenium. Puppies can safely be washed in shampoo.

*Mange.* This skin disease results from microscopic eight-legged spider-like creatures which cause loss of hair, great discomfort to the dog and occasionally coarsening of the skin. There are three types of mange: two of them attack the body of the animal, the other the ear.

Treatment is to replace the dog's bedding, thoroughly wash with a disinfectant around his sleeping area, and bathe the entire animal with liberal amounts of disinfectants and soapy water. Rinse him thoroughly and clean down the entire area you have been bathing him in. Repeat this every four days, but if the mange is still present after a couple of weeks consult your vet.

*Pneumonia.* This is a lung infection caused by either a virus, bacteria or worms. It is easily identified by a high body temperature, coughing and a general inertia in the dog. It is a serious disease and you should consult your vet. In the meantime, keep the dog warm and in a warm room with plenty of fresh air. Allow the dog to drink as much water as he likes.

*Rabies.* This is a virus disease, transmitted in the saliva of a rabid dog. It is a disease that brings death to all infected dogs and either, at worst, an agonizing death or, at best, a series of injections for infected humans.

Rabies is transmitted from dog to dog or to humans through a bite from an infected animal. Contraction of the disease can occur through contact with infected saliva through a skin wound.

The first symptom in dogs is agitation or extreme quiet. A friendly dog may become snappy, a snappy one subdued. Sexual excitement, frequent urination and total unpredictability may follow, with the virus eventually paralysing the nerves of the jaw and throat muscles. The jaw then hangs open and the dog, although thirsty, cannot swallow. Frothing at the mouth may occur. Once the brain is inflamed, the dog soon dies.

If, at any time, you or your dog come into contact with an infected animal – or even if you only suspect that you may have done so – consult your local doctor, veterinary officer and police.

**Left: The Irish Setter has a more elongated body and is more loose limbed than the English Setter. He is most attractive, with a rich mahogany-red coat. They are very friendly animals.**

*Ringworm.* This causes round, dry and scaly breaks in the skin on the chest and head which may eventually become infected with pus. The first step is to clip all hair around the infections and apply a solution of Cetavlon. In healthy dogs ringworm will disappear in about two months. This is a highly contagious disease so consult your vet.

*Shock.* Dogs can become shocked for a variety of reasons from a car accident to a haemorrhage and scalds. The animal becomes apathetic with a low temperature, a low pulse with rapid and shallow breathing, and a thirst. First aid consists of keeping the dog warm, allowing it full rest, and getting him to a vet.

*Ticks.* Dogs in country areas often encounter the sheep tick which is a blood-sucking parasite with a shiny body some 6–13mm ($\frac{1}{4}$–$\frac{1}{2}$in) in length.

Do not try to pull the tick out if its head is firmly in the dog. First, pour a little ether on a cottonwool pad and place it over the tick for about a minute. The tick will then withdraw its head and can be removed with a pair of tweezers.

*Worm infestations.* Several types of parasitic worms may try to use your dog as host, and it is especially during the first eight to nine months of his life that an infestation is most likely to occur. In the case of a young animal, worms can produce a variety of symptoms, including a pot belly, failure to grow normally and bad breath. Visual evidence is when the worms appear in the animal's faeces or vomit.

It is, of course, wise for all precautions to be taken against worms being transmitted to humans. Therefore do not encourage children to allow puppies to lick their faces and remember to wash hands before meals.

Most types of worm are not dangerous to dogs, but the round-worm may cause blindness in humans and is especially dangerous to children.

The treatment for worms is much more straightforward than it used to be, and does not now necessitate starving the animal. A safe worming concoction to use is Coopane. But do consult your vet before worming a dog, especially a pup.

If you bought your pup from a good kennel, he will already have been wormed at about six weeks. This entails two wormings, with an interval of two weeks. The adult worms are killed the first time, and the adults which have since hatched from eggs the second time. This is repeated again when the animal is five to six months old.

*Wounds.* Wounds are breaks in the skin of a dog's body. If superficial they will heal naturally, but if deep and torn they will need attention. If the dog is bleeding profusely, the first job is to stop the flow by placing a bandage or wad of cloth over the wound. If the wound is deep, call in a vet, but if it is slight apply a dressing as soon as the bleeding is reduced.

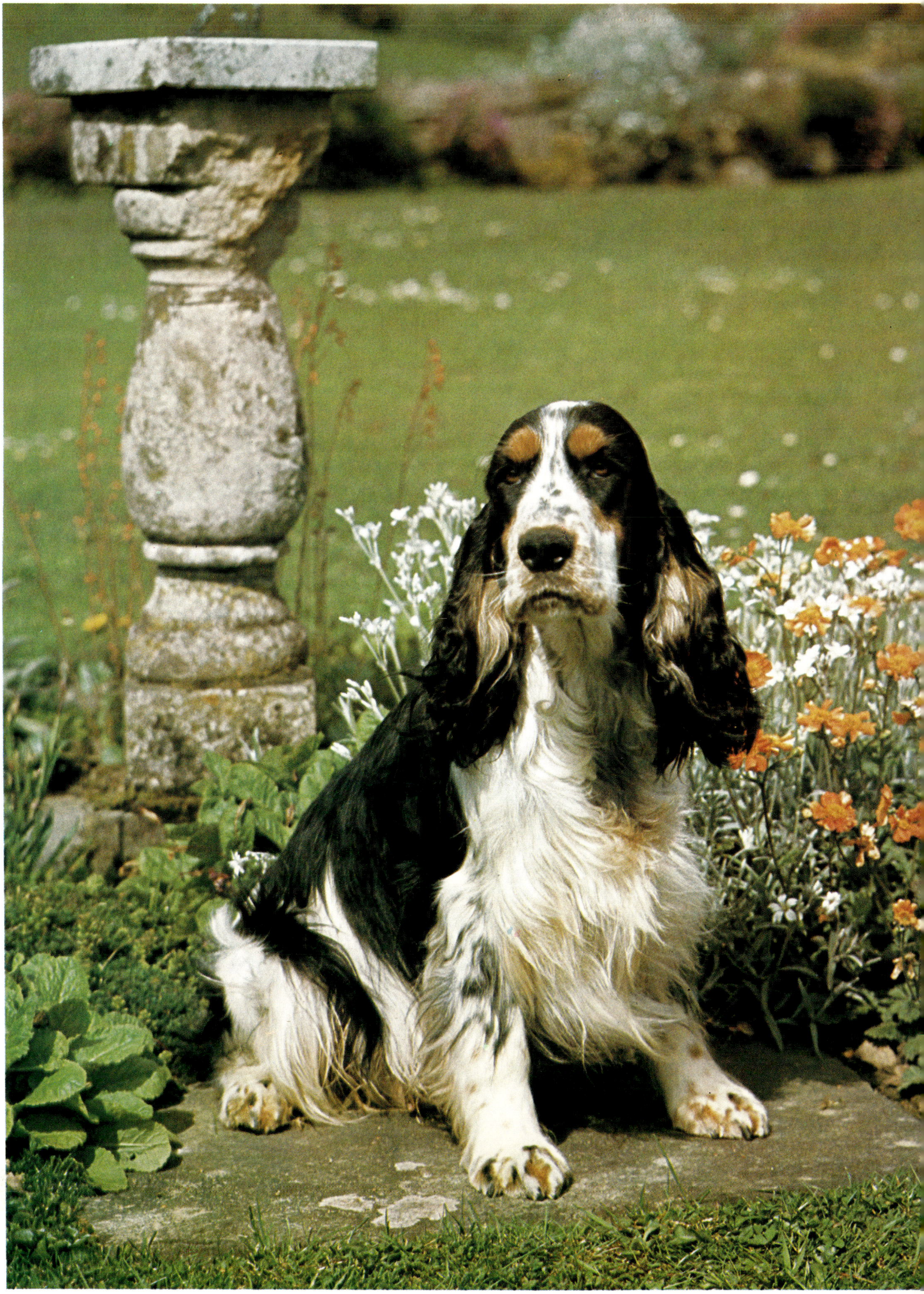

# Family dogs

A family dog is always something special and there is usually a small boy or girl it selects as a pal. It can be a large or a small dog, long or short, with or without a tail, excessively hairy or even bald, like the Mexican Hairless Dog. But whatever they look like, they all have one thing in common: they become part of the family.

Perhaps the chief characteristic that a good family dog requires is to be friendly and to like children. Many breeds are friendly, but there are some which are noted for their tolerance to children. These include most of the hounds (Bassets and Beagles), Spaniels, Collies, Old English Sheepdogs, gundogs (Retrievers and Setters), Pyreneans and Newfoundlands. There are, of course, many others.

The best family dogs are those which have grown up from their puppy stage with a house full of youngsters. If you take over a mature dog, staid in its ways and which has never lived with children, don't expect it to like being pulled around and wrestled with. It's not fair on the dog.

**A Bitch or a Dog?**

The question ofen arises as to whether a bitch would be more suitable as a family pet than a dog. Most people would agree that a bitch is more home loving and less tempted to roam, but much of the waywardness in dogs is due to bad training. A dog which is not allowed to roam the streets but given a comfortable home life, together with strict supervision and training when young, will not give you any problems. But once he has sampled the sweet life you will have trouble with him.

Left: The English Cocker Spaniel makes an excellent pet and companion, being one of the friendliest of dogs with a merry temperament and perpetually wagging his tail. Below: Although being friendly, this Boston Terrier should not be allowed to lick a child's face.

Left: The alert and attractive Dachshund is a native of Germany where, as the name implies, he was bred to go underground after badgers. This dog's powerful body and short legs enable him to enter a badger's earth and force a way through the tunnels of the set until coming to grips with the quarry or holding it at bay. There are three different coat varieties of Dachshund: smooth-haired, long-haired and wire-haired. There are also miniature varieties.
Right: The Wire-haired Dachshund has yet to become widely popular, although he is very appealing. With this type the shape is not so exaggerated as with the Long-haired and Smooth-haired Dachshunds. They have more of a terrier-like appearance.

The major difficulty with a bitch is to keep her home and away from dogs when she is in season (see 'Breeding puppies'). If you have children who might let a bitch out when in season, then do have a dog. It would be irresponsible to risk bringing unwanted pups into your home, with all its attendant expenses and difficulties, not least of which is to find good homes for the pups. If, however, she does get loose and is mated, take her immediately to your vet who will be able to give an injection to prevent her producing pups.

The bitch will come into season at six-monthly intervals, and for about eighteen to twenty-one days she will have to be kept away from the male of the species, although mating is possible for only three to five days. The rest of the time she will attract all the dogs in the neighbourhood if they scent her. Therefore when you take her for walks, and if she is small enough, carry her twenty or so paces from your front gate before letting her down. And when returning carry her a similar distance to your gate. This will prevent all the local dogs from wandering over your front garden.

Dabbing the bitch's paws with a strongly scented substance, such as oil of lavender, will help to put the dogs off the scent.

**Decreasing the Sexual Drive**
It is possible to make a dog's or bitch's life happier by removing their sexual drive. In the dog it will make him less prone to wandering and chasing the neighbourhood bitches, and with the bitch it will free

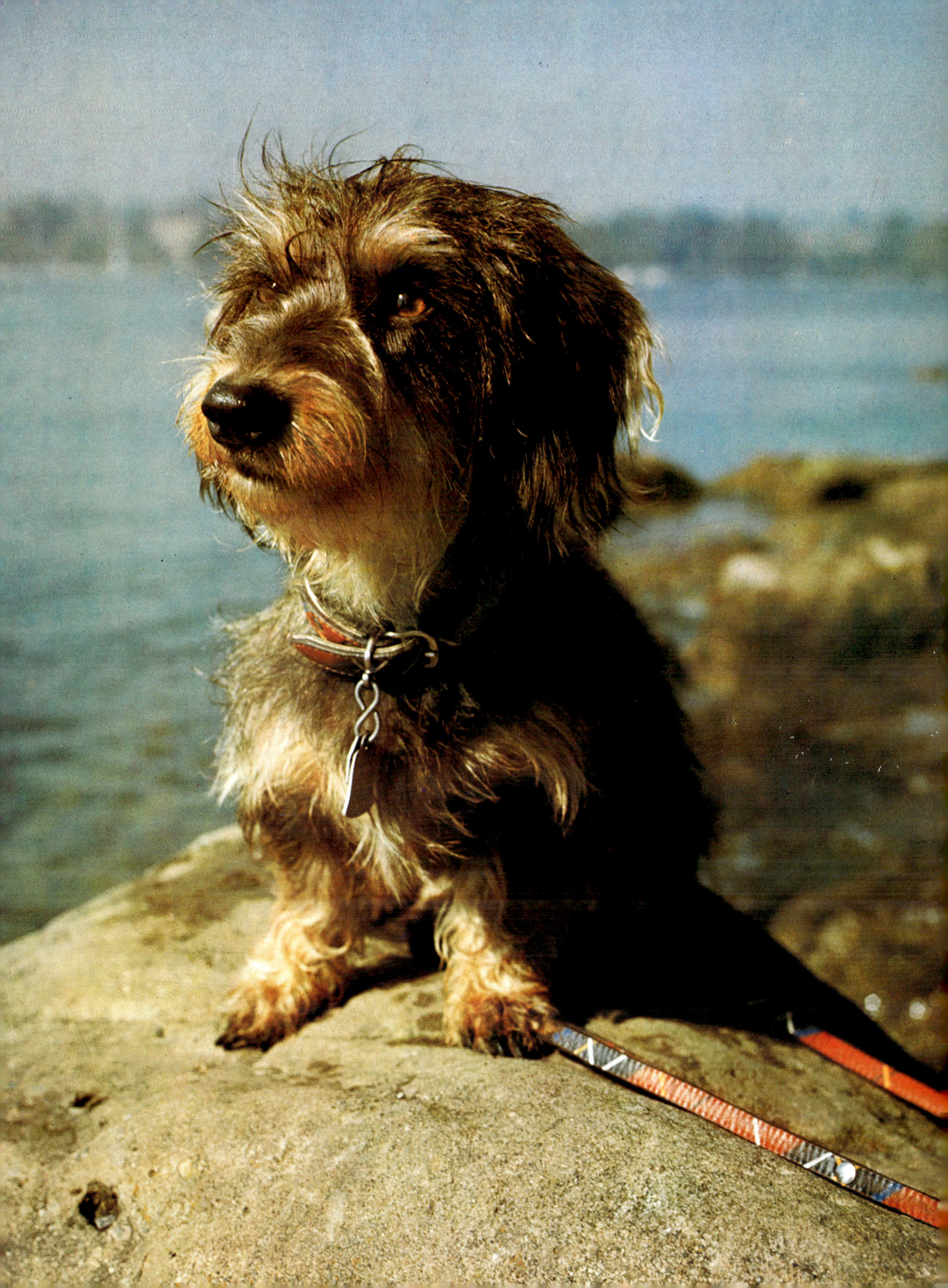

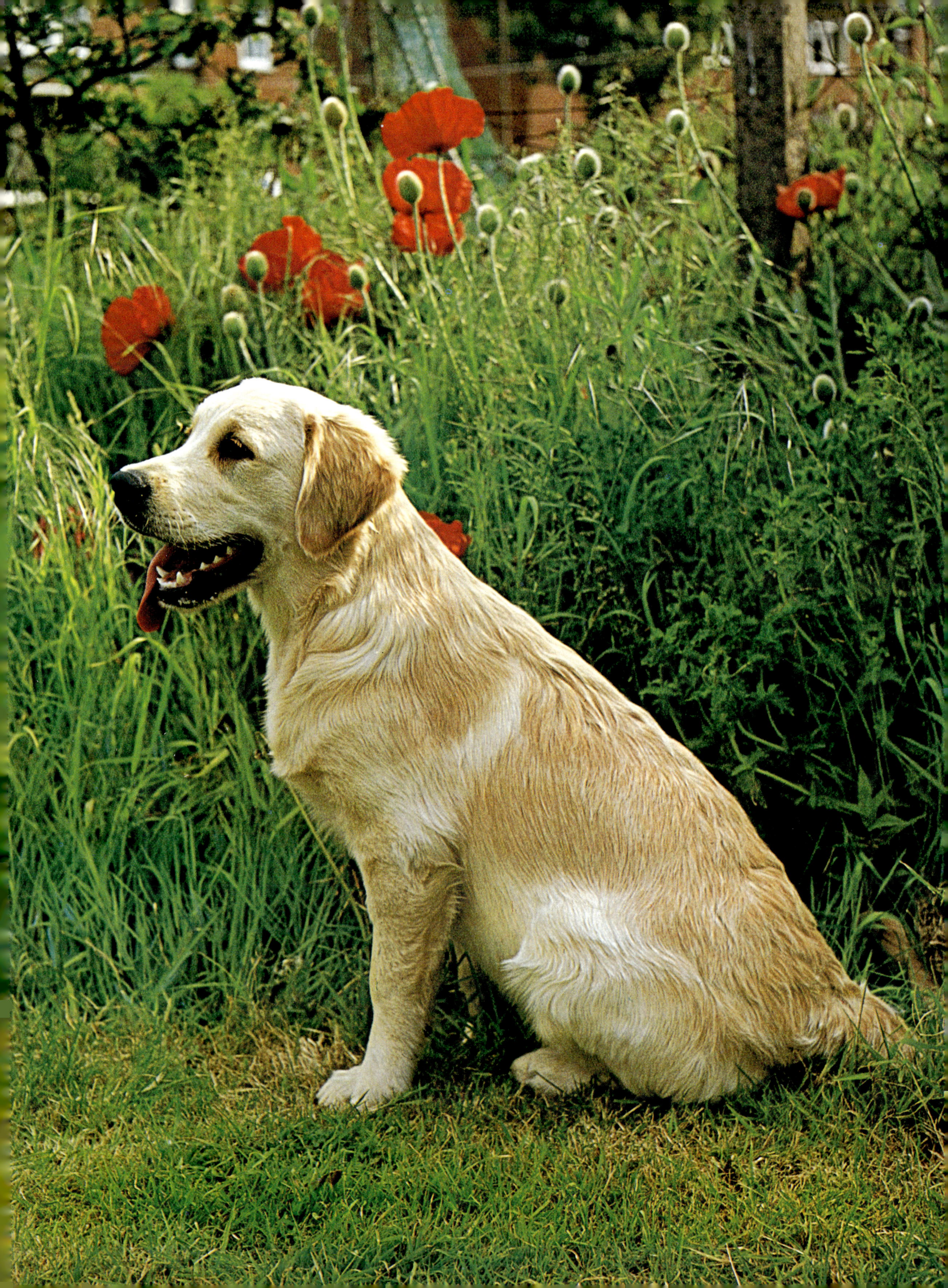

her, and you, from the problems that arise when she is in season.

The dog is castrated, but this must not be done before an age when he reaches sexual maturity. To do it before this time induces him to become extremely fat and lazy and he will tend to lose his character and initiative. A castrated dog can be a much happier fellow to have around the house as he loses his pack instinct and is less likely to fight other dogs.

Castration may be carried out as soon as he is sexually mature, which can be any time between the ages of six and eighteen months.

A bitch can undergo spaying (removal of the ovaries) as soon as she has been in season once, but here again ensure that it is not done too early or she may become fat. If it is carried out at the right time there will be no great change of character in her.

## What Breed Shall We Have?

The answer to this often depends on the size of your house and pocket – and how much exercise you can give the animal. It would not be fair to keep an Irish Wolfhound or a Saint Bernard in a high-rise flat or even in the suburbs of a large town or city. Animals of this size need a large house and regular exercise, and plenty of food. So if you are on a tight budget don't choose a large dog.

In between the largest and smallest breeds there are many suitable ones to choose from, as well as many delightful mongrels. But the drawback with a mongrel if bought as a puppy is that the dog he grows up to be can differ greatly from how you imagined him to look.

**Left: Golden Retrievers are among the most amiable dogs and make good family pets. Below: Beagles are lively dogs which may even form a protective attitude towards the family cat.**

Pedigree dogs are expensive, but when the cost is spread over the life of the animal it is well worth while. And there is the added bonus in that you will be able to show the dog in official dog shows, which are always a lot of fun for the dog and the owner.

To set out a long and extensive list of breeds suitable as family pets, which will make friends with children, play with them and protect them, is virtually impossible; so much depends on how a dog was trained when a pup. But there are happy dogs and aggressive ones and a potential owner does not have to be a canine expert to spot them. Have a good look at your friends' dogs and see which is the happiest and best natured. Make sure that he is not too big and ask how much food he eats, how much exercise is required, and if he is particularly susceptible to illness. All this information will be invaluable to ensure that you do not make the wrong decision and end up with a problem.

Once you have decided upon the breed, find out if there is a reputable kennel in your area which breeds them. If in doubt about finding a kennel, write to your national kennel club (enclosing a stamped and addressed envelope) for the name of the kennel in your area. And it is always worth having a chat with the kennel owner, saying that it is a family dog you want and one which will be good with youngsters.

Whether you decide upon a bitch or a dog, if it is treated well and looked after you will have a loyal family companion for ten, twelve, or even more years.

Below: These three Rough-coated Collies are intelligent and attractive dogs, whose name is said to derive from the Colley sheep. Right: The Dalmatian, otherwise known as the 'spotted Dick', 'fire house dog' or 'plum pudding dog' is distinctive and well known.

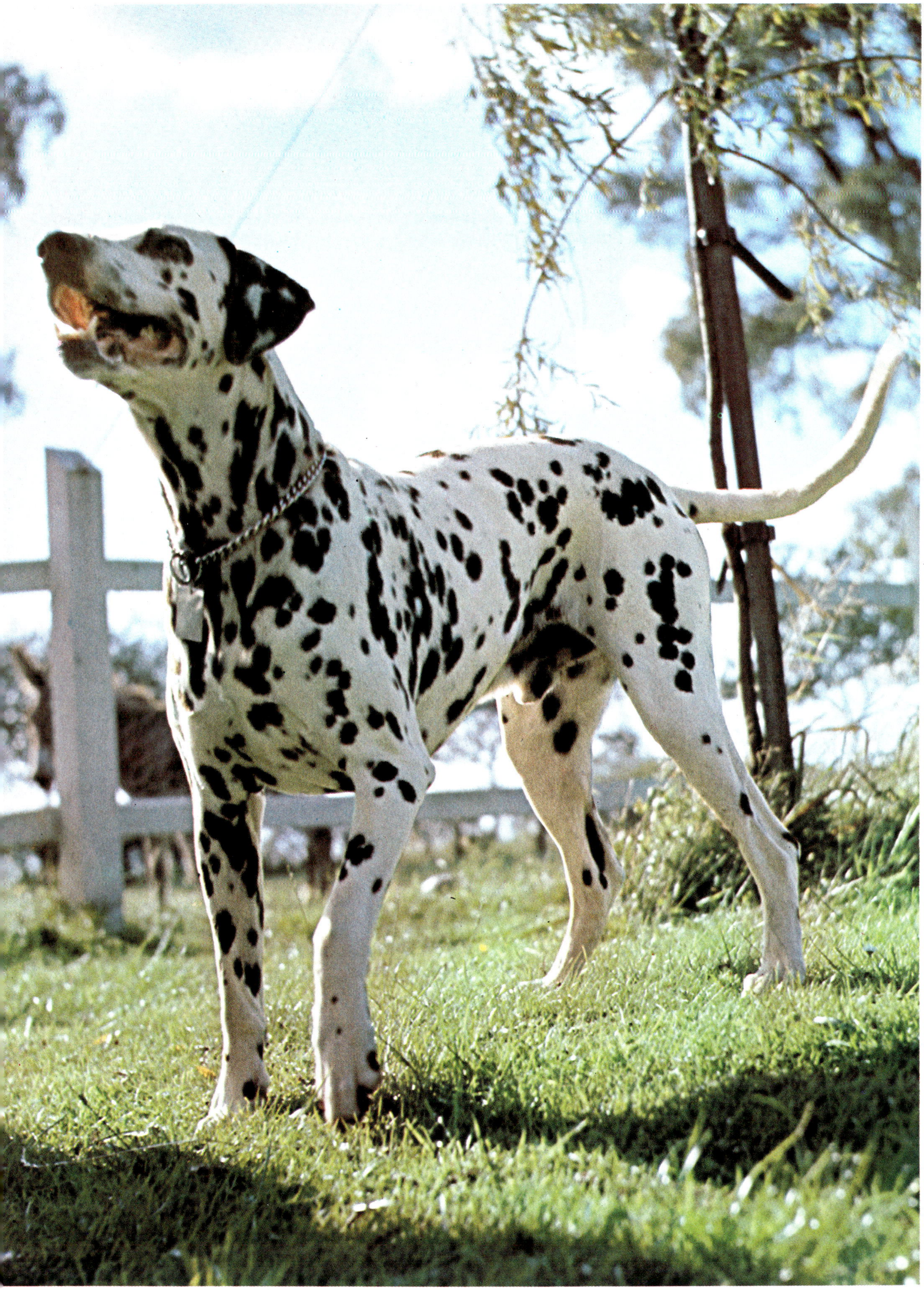

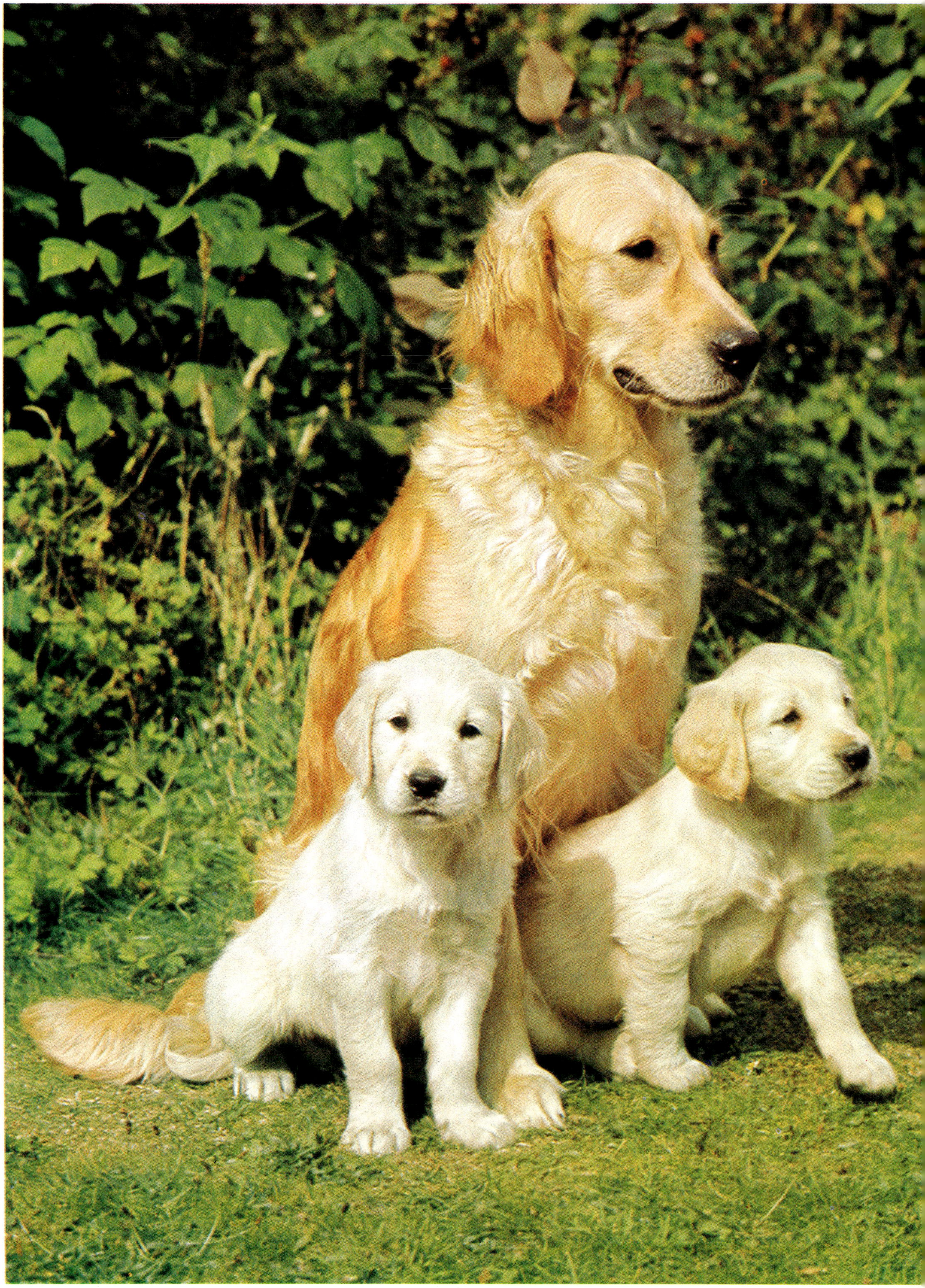

# Breeding puppies

The decision as to whether or not to breed from your bitch fundamentally depends if she is a pedigree. If her parentage is doubtful, then forget about raising pups from her. You'll find it's very difficult to get good homes for puppies not of a specific breed.

If the bitch is of a pedigree line and not less than fifteen months old and not more than five years she should be able to bear pups quite happily. However, do remember that a litter of pups can create quite a disturbance in a household, especially if it is cramped and there are a lot of children. If you have your bitch solely as a family pet, there may not be much point in disturbing both her and your family's daily routine. Also, there is always a slight risk present, so if you don't need pups don't breed from her.

The expense must also be considered. You may have to pay for the services of a good stud dog, and then there's the cost of feeding additional mouths for, perhaps, ten to twelve weeks – or longer. You will also have to bear the expense of injections and medical care. But whatever else, do not bring unwanted puppies into this world. In America alone there are estimated to be in excess of fifteen million unwanted dogs.

If someone tells you that it is advisable for a bitch to have a litter of pups at least once in her life, to guard against female illness in old age, then you can be assured that this is a fallacy that you can safely ignore. Many bitches live to an old age quite happily and healthily without ever bearing pups.

## Choosing a Mate

If you have a pedigree bitch, with all the records to prove it, you'll want to find a dog with similar pedigree. This often is not as easy as it sounds, unless he chances to be the dog next door.

Do ensure that the stud dog is what his owner claims. Ask to see the dog's pedigree credentials because you do not want to find yourself with unwanted pups nine weeks later, the indirect result of

Left: These attractive and lively young Golden Retriever puppies have a gun-dog's instinct. They enjoy being taught to retrieve, even if they are kept only as household pets. Right: Beagle puppies need space to play or they will not develop properly. Puppies kept in small pens in insanitary conditions are unable to follow their instincts to keep their bed clean. Often, this can create housetraining problems at a much later date.

some unrecorded mating by the stud dog's ancestors.

There are two good ways to find a good mate for your bitch. First, contact the breeder at the kennel from where you bought your bitch. He will be able to give you all the advice you need and may even offer the services of one of his stud dogs. Second, contact your national kennel club, who will supply you with information about breeders in your area (don't forget to enclose a stamped and addressed envelope).

What the owner of the dog may want in return for the dog's services is a matter for negotiation. It may be an outright fee, with the opportunity of a repeat if the first mating is unsuccessful, or to be able to select and keep one of the pups from the ensuing litter. It's all a matter of discussion between the two owners.

**The Bitch in Season**
A bitch comes into season twice in a year, at six-month intervals, and it is only at these times that she is receptive to amorous overtures. Indeed, it is only at these times that she, as a bitch, is attractive to the male of the species.

There are, by the way, several expressions in use to describe when a bitch is receptive to the male, from the technical term 'oestral period' to 'in season' and 'on heat'. Of these I prefer to use 'in season'.

A bitch will have her first season some time between the ages of six and ten months, usually about the eighth. The signs of this are restlessness, perhaps increased passing of water and a swelling of her external sex organ, the vulva, which lasts for five to seven days. This is followed by a reddish discharge, which slowly turns pinkish, lasting between four and seven days.

As the discharge subsides, the bitch becomes receptive to the dog and it is at this stage that mating should take place. This receptive state is during the second week of the bitch being in season and lasts for three to five days. After this short period she will not be receptive.

Left: The Sealyham is an active dog. His proficiency is in badger hunting and digging, yet at the same time he makes a delightful companion and pet. He is a strong and powerfully-built Terrier and his coat is hard and more abundant than that of a Wire Fox Terrier. Right: It is not unusual for a Saint Bernard to have ten or more puppies in a litter. Feeding so many puppies is an expensive business and their diet has to be more than adequate to ensure that they maintain the necessary growth rate. Dogs such as the Saint Bernard have a massive bone structure and calcium and vitamin supplements to their food are often necessary.

**The Mating**
The bitch should be wormed twice, at fourteen-day intervals, just before mating is due. It is usual on the day of the mating for the bitch to be taken to the dog, to ensure that he feels relaxed and at ease. If the dog is an experienced stud dog and the bitch has previously produced a litter, then it all can be left to the two animals. But if the mating is between a novice dog and a maiden bitch, which is very unwise, it is advisable to ensure that an experienced breeder is present. In any case, the owners should be there to encourage and calm their animals.

During mating, the bitch and dog will be held firmly together when the dog's penis swells inside the female. No attempt should be made to prise the two animals apart. Eventually, the dog will be able to withdraw his penis, quite naturally.

**Pregnancy**
From the date when the bitch is fertilized, which is usually one or two days after mating, she will produce a litter of puppies in sixty-three days.

Many people count this period from the day of mating, but this is wrong. It often takes a day or so for the eggs in the bitch to be fertilized following mating.

Most bitches give birth slightly early, but if her time goes over sixty-three days, call a vet.

During pregnancy special attention must be given to her diet. She will need smaller meals, more often, as her stomach is really quite small and if distended with food it could interfere with the pups and also cause her discomfort. Provide her with more proteins and less carbohydrates. Do consult your vet about her diet and if she has not had pups before ask him to attend the birth, in case complications arise.

Don't treat her as an invalid and do give her regular and gentle exercise, with plenty of opportunity to rest and be quiet. Do not let children chase her around.

Two charming Golden Retriever puppies.

49

She will need a large box in which to have the pups, and this should be at least one-and-a-half times her own length, preferably larger. It should be draught-proof, warm and with high back and side pieces, with a frame 150 mm (6 in) high along the front to prevent the pups from falling out.

Towards the end of pregnancy, about the fiftieth day, her breasts will be swollen, full of milk ready for the youngsters. Her teats will be enlarged. At the end she will pant a great deal for breath and will probably go off her food. Ensure that she has plenty of clean drinking water. A sure sign that the puppies are due is when she scratches and moves the blankets in her box to form a nest.

This is an anxious moment for bitches, especially if they have not given birth previously. Be patient with her and try to reassure her that you are there to give comfort and help. Experienced bitches will probably cause no problem and worry to you. They will produce the pups, one at a time, at intervals ranging from a few minutes to a couple of hours, tearing open the opaque bag in which each pup is born and also severing the umbilical cord.

The bitch normally cleans up each pup before directing it to a nipple and this is achieved before a fresh pup is born. The main concern is to keep the pups warm and the bitch will normally see to this.

## The Care of the Bitch

For the first twenty-four hours after the pups are born feed the bitch a milky diet every four hours. Add glucose to the milk. By now she should have been given penicillin injections, which will ensure that she is free from any infection, especially if she has eaten the afterbirth. Normally, two injections of penicillin are required, one as soon as all the pups are born, the other the day after.

From then and until the pups are weaned, at about five to six weeks, she will require a high protein diet three times a day, plus a snack at night.

## Worming the Pups

At about six weeks the pups must be wormed, repeating it two weeks later. This is because the adult worms are killed the first time, but not the eggs. The second worming kills the eggs which have subsequently hatched into adults. This worming treatment should be repeated when the pups are five to six months old.

## Leaving Mother

When about ten to twelve weeks old it is time for each pup to leave the comfort and safety of his home with his mother, and by this time most bitches are pleased to be rid of them.

Far left: Plenty of sleep is essential for the good health and growth of puppies. These Foxhound puppies appear to be very wary of the world.
Left: In some breeds the adult dog may bear little resemblance to the puppy. This dark brown and white Bearded Collie puppy may end up as light in colour as its mother.
Below: Dogs of the Spitz type are the working dogs of northern latitudes. This Norwegian bitch suckles her litter on a farm in between her work, which can be anything from driving cows out to pasture, accompanying the farmer when shooting, to guarding the farmyard against intruders.

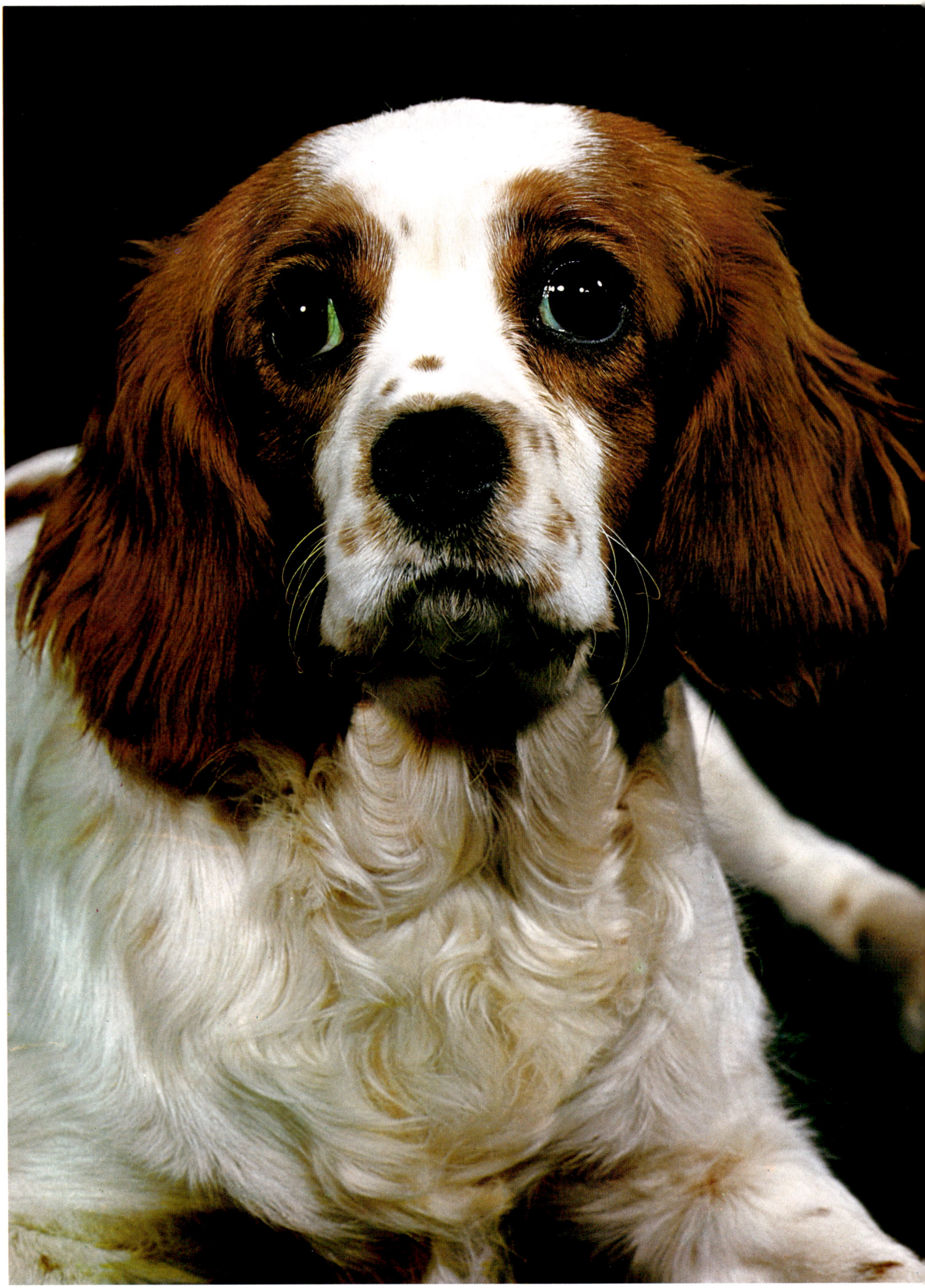

# Toy breeds and other small dogs

To most people, toy dogs must seem noisy and precocious animals, rather than real dogs. But this is not so. They are specific and highly distinctive breeds developed solely for pleasure. They make admirable pets and companions and are excellent as watchdogs.

Just because they are dainty and diminutive, you should not assume that they are devoid of intelligence and courage. Often, for their size, they exhibit far more sense and fortitude than giant dogs.

Toy dogs are not new. The ancestors of the Pekingese, for instance, can be traced back more than 2000 years when to the Chinese emperors they were known as Lion Dogs.

Toy dogs gained popularity after World War II, when many people wanted small dogs which would be happy in a small house. And as food was – and still is – expensive, it is obviously cheaper to feed a small dog than a Bloodhound or even a Spaniel. But because they are cheaper to feed, don't think that they are automatically cheap to buy. Often it is quite the reverse. Toy bitches tend to have fewer pups in a litter and there is always a great demand for them.

If you do decide to buy a toy dog, but are unsure as to the range of breeds, the best answer is to go along to a large dog show, possibly a championship where you will be able to gain a first-hand impression of them. There are breeds to suit all tastes, from the miniature Pug to the Black-and-tan Terrier and more ornate and dainty dogs such as Papillons and Chihuahuas.

These toy dogs, of course, have small stomachs and

**Left: The Cavalier King Charles Spaniel** is a very old breed, closely associated with the King Charles Spaniel. The Cavaliers have longer noses than the King Charles type and tend to be more sporting. **Right: This Toy Poodle** has all the charm of a very small dog, combined with the fun-loving acrobatic ability of its larger relations. However, like all the dogs in the Poodle group, toys carry a very heavy coat. It must be clipped at regular intervals and brushed and combed daily to prevent the formation of mats that cannot be untangled.

it is essential that they should not be overfed. Several small meals a day is far better than a single large one. Toy dogs do have a tendency to develop bad teeth, but this can be remedied by giving them large bones to chew, together with dog biscuits.

**The Main Toy Breeds**
*Black-and-tan Terrier.* This breed is also known as the English Toy Terrier and owes much of its origin to the Manchester Terrier. Small pups were selected and bred until the hardy, alert, quick and energetic toy terrier was produced. But beware, he does have a tendency to bark at every sound, and if you live in an apartment or in close proximity to other people, this can be a continual annoyance.

In good examples of this breed the head and skull should be long, flat and narrow, level and wedge-shaped without cheekiness. The eyes must be small and bright.

His coat is close, smooth, short and glossy and in show dogs it must be jet black and rich mahogany in colour.

*Chihuahua.* This is the tiniest dog in the world and seems to have been derived from a terrier of the black-and-tan type crossed with the small Mexican temple dog, which was a native breed at the time Cortes invaded Central America. Indeed, it is recorded that the ancestors of the Chihuahua lived wild and untamed in the mountains of Mexico, living on small rodents and young birds as well as other food. They have even been said to have roamed in packs of fifty or more, hunting wild pigs. Their activity and liveliness make them excellent dogs for the home.

Above: The Maltese is a dog with a long history. He is known to have been a great favourite with the ladies of nobility of Rome and Greece. They are beautiful and intelligent dogs, popular on both sides of the Atlantic.
Right: The Brussels Griffon is a toy dog small in size but big in personality. He is one of the most humorous and cheeky toy dogs. Sometimes he is known as the Griffon Bruxellois.

There are two varieties, the smooth-coated and the long-coated. Both of them are delightful. They are essentially house dogs who love to play a major role with the family. Although Chihuahuas like warmth, they do enjoy a scamper across meadows.

Feeding them does not offer any problem. Two small meals a day are quite sufficient, giving 55–85 gm (2–3 oz) of food at each meal. They will eat vegetables as well as meat.

*Griffon.* There are two varieties of this distinctive dog. The Griffon Bruxellois is a rough-coated dog, while the Petit Brabançon is the smooth-coated type. However, they are usually classified under the heading Griffon.

They are smart, alert and very jolly dogs, quite easy to train. They vary a great deal in size, from 1.3–4.5 kg (3–10 lb), but the most desirable weigh 2.7–4.0 kg (6–9 lb).

Their ancestors can be traced back a long way, as far as the fifteenth century, and one is pictured in a painting of that time by Jan van Eyck, called *Giovanni Arnolfini and His Bride*.

The dog we know today is from a cross between the Belgian Sheepdog and the German Affenpinscher. The Griffon increased in popularity in 1870 when he was a favourite with the Belgian queen.

Griffons thrive on a diet chiefly of meat. Two meals a day are sufficient for adults.

*Italian Greyhound.* This is a true, miniature greyhound. He is a beautiful and fascinating animal, developed from a small greyhound.

As his name indicates, he comes from Italy where he is called Piccola Lavriere Italiana. His lineage goes back a long way and he is known to have existed in the same form for over 2000 years. In his time he has been a great favourite with Roman, Greek and Egyptian nobility.

He was a great favourite with painters and royalty, such as Charles I, Frederick the Great and Queen Victoria. By the late 1800s he reached the peak of his popularity.

They are graceful and elegant dogs at play and it is a joy to watch them. Although they look so fragile they are active and delight in a run during winter.

Italian Greyhounds are very gentle and affectionate, and this is probably why they were so loved by ladies. It is essential not to overfeed them.

*Japanese.* Japanese Spaniels originated in China about 500 BC and travelled to Europe by way of Japan. They arrived in Japan as the result of an excellent pair of them being given to the Mikado by an emperor of China. The dogs arrived in England when Commodore Perry gave a brace to Queen Victoria.

These delightful dogs are in many ways similar to the Pekingese. They are lively with an extremely delicate appearance, being high spirited, happy and intelligent. They are easily trained.

Japanese dogs make excellent apartment and small house dogs, showing great loyalty. But do ensure that they are not subjected to extremely cold weather nor to rapid changes in temperature.

*King Charles Spaniel.* It is thought that this breed was developed by crossing the short-nosed miniature breeds from China with Maltese dogs. The King Charles Spaniel was, of course, a great favourite of King Charles II of England, after whom they are named. But they were known in England as far back as King Henry VIII and were mentioned by Queen Elizabeth I's physician. King Charles I also owned one, but it is certainly his son, Charles II, who made them popular.

They were more or less banned at the English

Above: The Papillon has large fringed ears, resembling the wings of a butterfly – as the French name implies – and the common, well defined white blaze on the face is taken to represent the body of the insect. Left: The diminutive Yorkshire Terrier has a short and fluffy coat which will grow to floor length, with a fine silky texture. They are high spirited dogs delighting in rushing about in true terrier fashion, and this makes them popular dogs. Right: The Pug first came to Britain through Dutch traders from the Dutch East India Company. The breed became very fashionable with ladies of nobility. They are intelligent dogs, anxious to please their owners.

Court after the fall of the Stuarts, but happily they were still kept in many country houses. They later returned to popularity during Victorian times, when Queen Victoria favoured them. Indeed, a King Charles named Dash was a companion and plaything to the royal children. They are very affectionate little dogs, wonderful with children and good in the home.

Their general appearance is compact and refined, with a deep and wide chest, short and straight legs and a short and level back.

With regard to the colour of their coats there are four separate varieties. The King Charles itself is black-and-tan; the Prince Charles, white, black-and-tan; the Blenheim, red and white; and the Ruby, red.

*Cavalier King Charles Spaniel.* This is a very old breed and its ancestry is closely associated with the King Charles Spaniel. When King Charles Spaniels were being selected and bred, it became fashionable to produce dogs with short noses. The line with the longer nose, fine-pointed muzzle and flat-topped skull disappeared and very little was seen of them for about a hundred years.

Then, in about 1930, a small group of dedicated breeders decided to revive and reintroduce the true and old type of King Charles Spaniel. To distinguish it from the King Charles Spaniel it was given the name Cavalier.

These dogs are by nature very anxious to please their masters and are more sporting than the King Charles Spaniel.

*Maltese.* This miniature dog has a history stretching back 3000 years. He was a strong favourite with ladies of nobility of Rome and Greece.

They are beautiful and intelligent dogs, although not currently enjoying great popularity. This may be because prospective owners think they are difficult to keep clean and well groomed. But they are no more a problem than other long-haired dogs.

*Miniature Pinscher.* This breed owes his parentage to the German Herr Dobermann, who produced the Dobermann Pinscher.

The miniature Pinscher is a well balanced, sturdy dog with a compact smooth coat. He is full of life and vigour, always out to impress people. His aggression and over-confidence often make him difficult to train.

*Papillon.* This breed derives its name from the fact that properly carried ears should suggest an open-winged butterfly. The breed was so famous at one time that many ladies would not have their portraits painted unless one of these charming dogs was on her lap. Rubens and Watteau painted the breed many times.

He is a lively dog, but not robust and so must be fed carefully. He is very susceptible to cold weather.

*Pekingese.* This is a very ancient breed, dating back some 2000 years to ancient China, when they were known as Lion Dogs. They were brought to England by soldiers after the English looted the Imperial Palace at Peking.

They are certainly the most popular of the toy breeds, exhibiting great dignity, beauty, intelligence and adaptability. They are full of fun and very active.

*Pomeranian.* This dog owes its name to Pomerania, a former province of north-east Germany, now mostly in north-west Poland, where it was bred. It is a member of the Spitz group of dogs, which is admirably demonstrated by its massive upstanding coat, pricked ears and tail curled over its back.

The breed became popular during the 1870s and its standing in the dog world was enhanced when Queen Victoria of England had one.

He is an excellent dog for small houses and apartments at the same time being active, intelligent and very obedient. He will, however, have to be

trained early or he may impose his will on the house.
*Pug.* This breed owes its origination to China. It is thought that Dutch traders from the Dutch East India Company brought dogs from China and introduced them to England in 1884. The breed became very fashionable with ladies of nobility.

Pugs are intelligent and delightful dogs, very anxious to please their owners, to whom they give complete allegiance.

They are often inclined to be greedy and to put weight on easily, so a close watch must be kept on their diet.

*Yorkshire Terrier.* This attractive and sporting little dog is truly English. His origin is not clearly known as records of his breeding were not kept, but he appears to be a descendant of the old Black-and-tan Terrier and the Skye Terrier. He became fashionable towards the end of the 1800s and happily is still popular today.

**Other Small Dogs**
In addition to the dogs formally classified as toys, there are other small breeds which are just as attractive and make very good pets for small homes and apartments.

*Affenpinscher.* This delightful little dog was known in Europe back in the seventeenth century. The name Affenpinscher in German means 'monkey terrier' and the breed we know today goes back to 1900. He is related to the Miniature Pinscher and the Griffon Bruxellois, making him a haughty, proud and very intelligent little dog. This often makes training difficult unless he is firmly controlled.

It is the nature of his coat that gives him his 'monkey-terrier' nick-name. The coat is short and dense in certain parts and shaggy and much longer in others. The coat is much longer and shaggier on the legs and around the eyes, nose and chin, giving the monkey appearance.

He makes a good guard dog, with a sharp bark and the courage of a lion. He still has the instinct of a terrier and will chase most things.

*Australian Silky Terrier.* This Australian terrier is from a cross between the Yorkshire Terrier and the Australian Terrier and is one of the best loved Australian dogs.

He is full of energy, being tireless and rather yappy, but a good companion and family dog. For preference he should weigh 3.6–4.5 kg (8–10 lb) and be 230 mm (9 in) high at the shoulder.

*Chinese Crested Dog.* Hairless dogs have always been among the rarest and most bizarre of all breeds. The only one to have made itself very popular is the Chinese Crested Dog, which is now becoming better known. Indeed, it is increasingly exhibited at dog shows.

The head carries a crest of flowing hair and there is hair on the feet and a plume on the end of the tail. Except for these hairy areas, the dog is naked. The colour of the skin varies quite a lot, but is usually mottled, like the bark on a plane tree. The skin is fine and silky to touch.

The reason for this hairlessness is not understood. However, without the protection afforded by a coat of hair it becomes necessary to shield the dog from strong sunlight and extremes of temperature.

Like all rarities, the Chinese Crested Dog is difficult to find and very expensive to buy.

*Jack Russell Terrier.* This attractive and lively little dog owes its breeding and lineage to a famous dog breeder from Devon, England: Parson Jack Russell. Indeed, Jack Russell was so well known in the dog world that he sat as a member on one of the first

Far left: Five attractive Pomeranians. These dogs owe their name to Pomerania, a former province of north-east Germany now mostly in north-west Poland, where the breed originated. They make excellent little dogs for small houses and apartments, being active, intelligent and obedient. Above: The Pekingese is a toy dog with great dignity and a high degree of stubbornness. Left: A Japanese Spaniel is longer legged than the Pekingese and has a beautiful flowing coat and curly plumed tail.

*Miniature Bull Terrier.* These very much resemble the normal Bull Terrier, except that they have a height not more than 355 mm (14 in) and a weight under 9 kg (20 lb).

He is a dog, although small, that requires plenty of exercise – two good walks a day as well as romping around the garden.

*Miniature Long-haired Dachshund.* This most attractive dog is highly intelligent and gay in mood, as well as being alert and bold. He should be a replica of his larger counterpart, but weighing not more than 5 kg (11 lb) and for preference 3–4 kg (7–9 lb).

The coat should be soft and straight, or only slightly waved, being at its longest under the neck and underparts of the body and behind the legs.

*Miniature Smooth-haired Dachshund.* As with the Miniature Long-haired Dachshund, this is just a miniature version of its larger namesake. For preference, its weight should not exceed 5 kg (11 lb). They are quite gentle dogs, even though they might put on a bold appearance.

*Miniature Poodle.* These are exact counterparts of their larger cousins, being very active, intelligent and elegant looking. The height at the shoulder for Miniature Poodles is 375 mm (15 in) and that for Toy Poodles 11 inches and under.

They are very chic little dogs. It was during the 1950s that they became world famous and since that

committees of the British Kennel Club, helping to clean up the dog-show business. (Faking and other malpractices were prevalent during the 1870s.)

The first Jack Russell Terriers were far different from the dog we know today, being much larger, somewhere between 375 and 400 mm (15 and 16 in) high and with a very long back.

The present day Jack Russell Terriers are much smaller, not more than 250 mm (10 in) high at the shoulder and less than 4.5 kg (10 lb) in weight.

Jack Russells tend to be mischievous little imps, keen on digging holes and even investigating those already dug. Indeed, he was bred from a stock delighting in digging out vermin and scratching at burrows.

Left: The Italian Greyhound is the smallest member of the Greyhound group. Claimed as a very ancient breed, it appears in many Renaissance paintings. He is lively and a keen hunter requiring plenty of exercise. He is particularly lean with a smooth coat that requires no more grooming than a rub down with a duster. Furthermore, he does not have a 'doggy' odour, and so is an excellent pet for the home.

time they have been improved in temperament. They are not now so nervous and neurotic. It is always wise before buying a small poodle to check on the parents and establish if they are neurotic.

They are dogs that like to have an audience when performing their tricks and if treated in an active way they are excellent pets. If they are kept solely to lay upon the owner's lap, then you will have a neurotic dog to cope with.

One great advantage with poodles is that they do not continually shed their coat over the carpets and furniture. But they do require careful clipping and trimming as otherwise they look a mess. Also, they have the tendency to develop hair around their ears, which must be regularly removed.

Although it is possible to clip poodles at home, it is always best to have it done professionally. For home clipping a pair of electric clippers are required, but there is always the danger of nipping the dog's body or causing clipper rash, due to heavy-handed clipping.

Clipping can begin when the puppy is only nine or ten weeks old and all that is necessary at that stage is to trim the tail, face and feet, but as the coat gets longer it will need lightly clipping to produce an even coat.

There are several well-known patterns of clips, such as Cowboy, Dutch and Lamb. Your local dog-clipping parlour will be able to show you pictures of the various styles and suggest which would best suit the age of your animal and the colour of his coat.

To get the best result from the clipping, give the dog a bath a day or so before the visit to the dog parlour. To maintain the dog in good shape, clipping must be done whenever he looks the slightest bit scruffy.

*Miniature Schnauzer*. The large schnauzer is a powerfully built, sinewy and robust dog with a square appearance. The Miniature Schnauzer is an exact replica, with a height to the shoulder of 330 mm (13 in) for bitches and 355 mm (14 in) for dogs.

He is an unusual dog, with a square look, a deep chest and short back. He is full of character, being bold, intelligent and very reliable. It is a breed that often shows up well in obedience tests.

They are dogs that grow very quickly, even the miniature, and need to be well fed. They also have the bonus of being very easy to housetrain.

Right: The Chinese Crested dog is an unforgettable dog. Except for a plume of hair on the tail, a little hair above the feet and the crest on the head, the dog is naked. The skin colour is usually mottled, resembling the bark of a plane tree. Because he does not have hair on his body he must be protected from extremes of cold and sunburn.

Right: Chihuahuas are extremely small dogs, weighing as little as ½ kg (1 lb). They are an ancient breed originating from Mexico and it is said that their ancestors have been known to hunt in packs. Their liveliness makes them excellent little dogs for the home.

61

# Sporting and hunting breeds

If dogs had not been invented, it is possible that man would have had to train some other animal to accompany him when pursuing his hunting and sporting activities. But man, with his infinite perspicacity, used dogs to his own advantage by tailoring them to suit his needs. Dogs of various shapes and sizes were forthcoming, either by natural selection by the dog for its mates, or by selective breeding of the animals by man.

It has evolved, quite logically, that dogs with short legs – and so lacking speed – track their quarry through an ability to follow a scent, while long-legged dogs are more able to give chase through being able to see their foe clearly. The point is further made by the fact that large dogs with good eyesight do not pursue badgers down dark holes; that job is left to the short-legged Dachshund and Terriers.

Archaeological evidence reveals that man has used dogs in sport and hunting for literally thousands of years. The Ancient Egyptians and Assyrians used dogs to run down their quarry. In such cases the dogs had to be both fleet of foot and aggressive, as the dogs killed the prey.

The killing was left to the dogs because man of those times could not keep up with them. But as man got himself mobile on the backs of horses, the picture changed dramatically. He could then keep up with the dogs and only needed them to track the prey.

With the advent of muzzle-loading sporting guns it was obvious that man was in need of a new type of dog, with reactions to enhance the advantages of his new 'toy'. The new dog turned out to be the Pointer, which

**Left:** This English Springer Spaniel is popular in both Britain and the USA. This dog is awaiting the command to retrieve.
**Right:** A mixed pack of dogs in pursuit of rabbits.

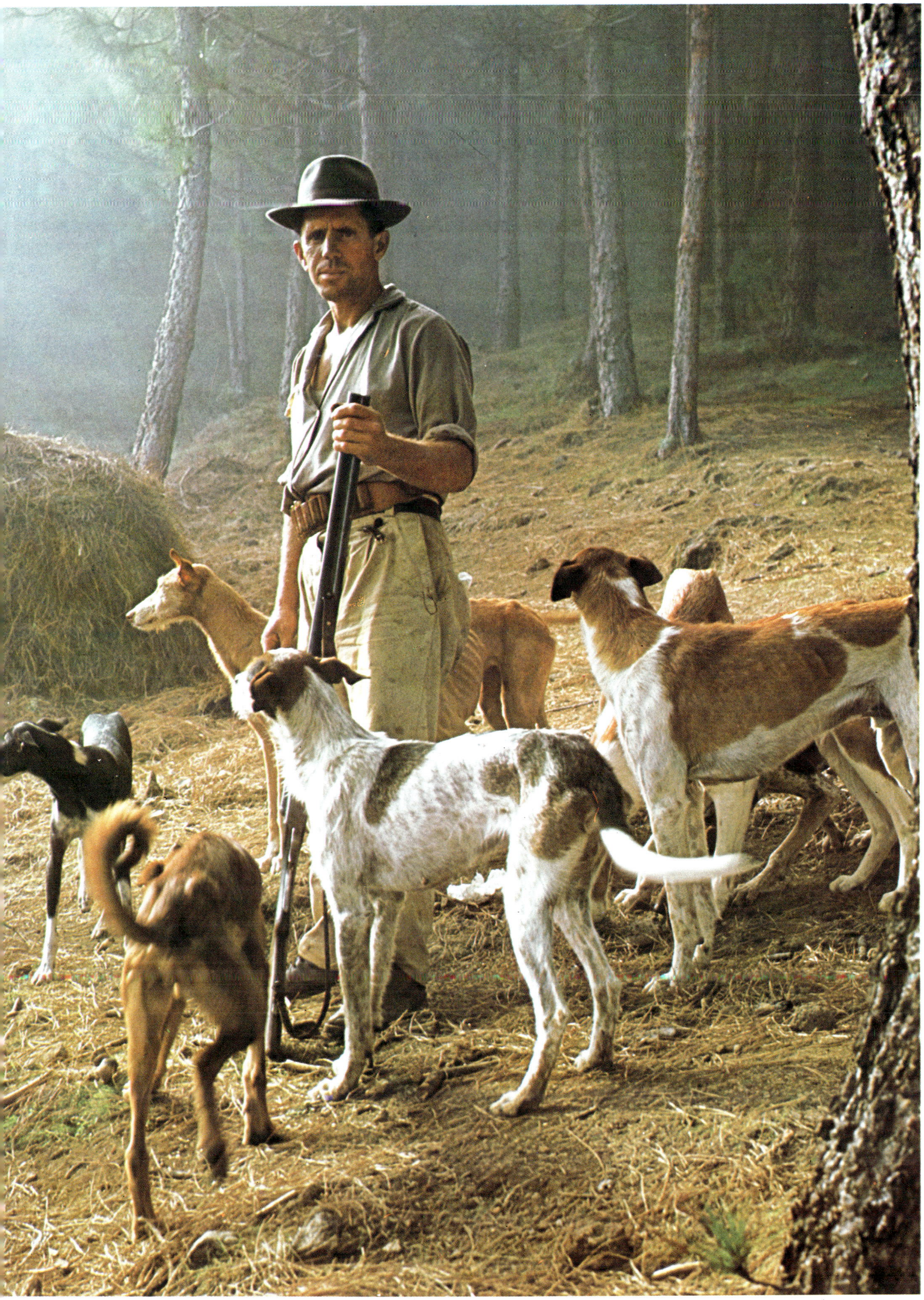

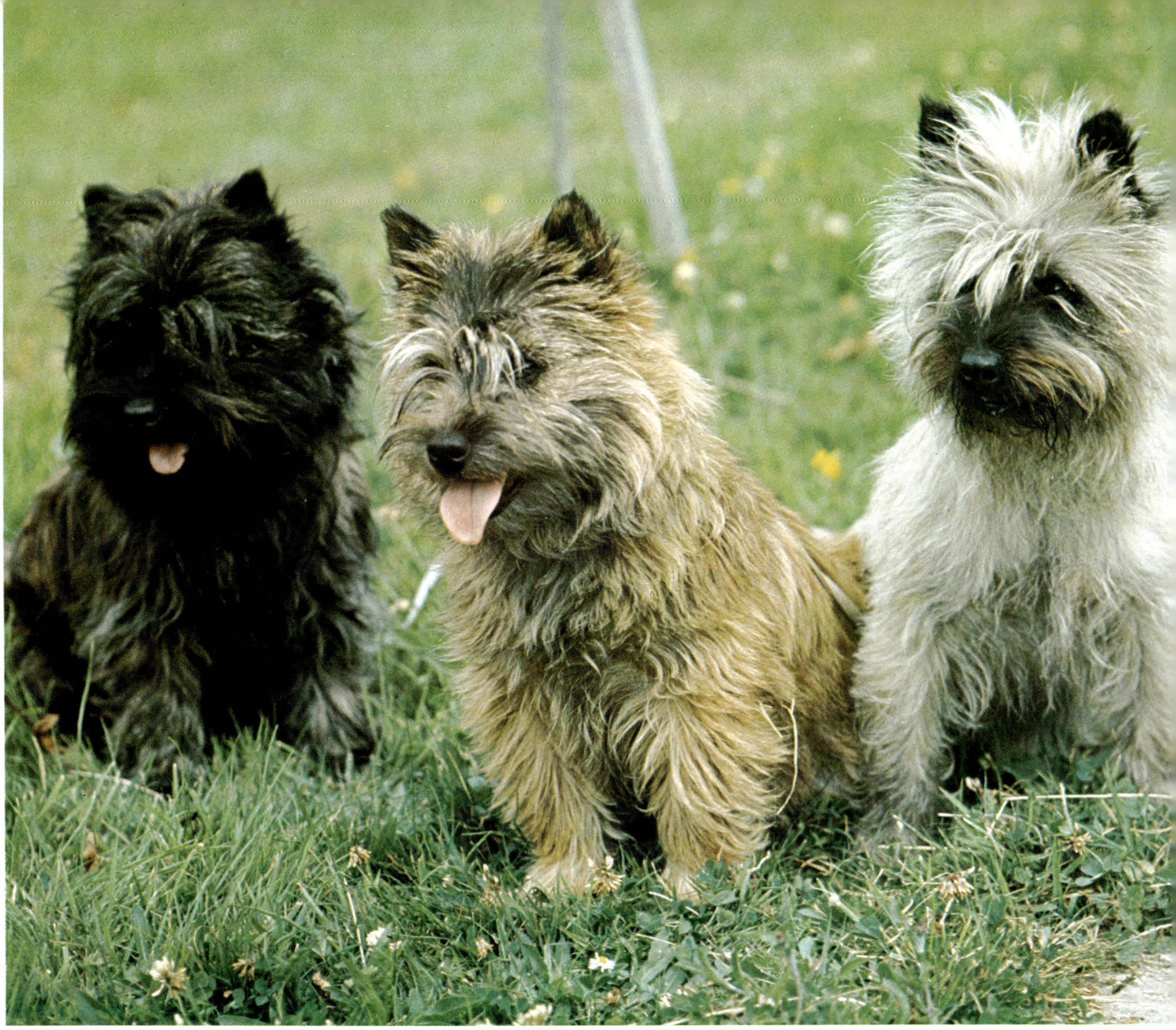

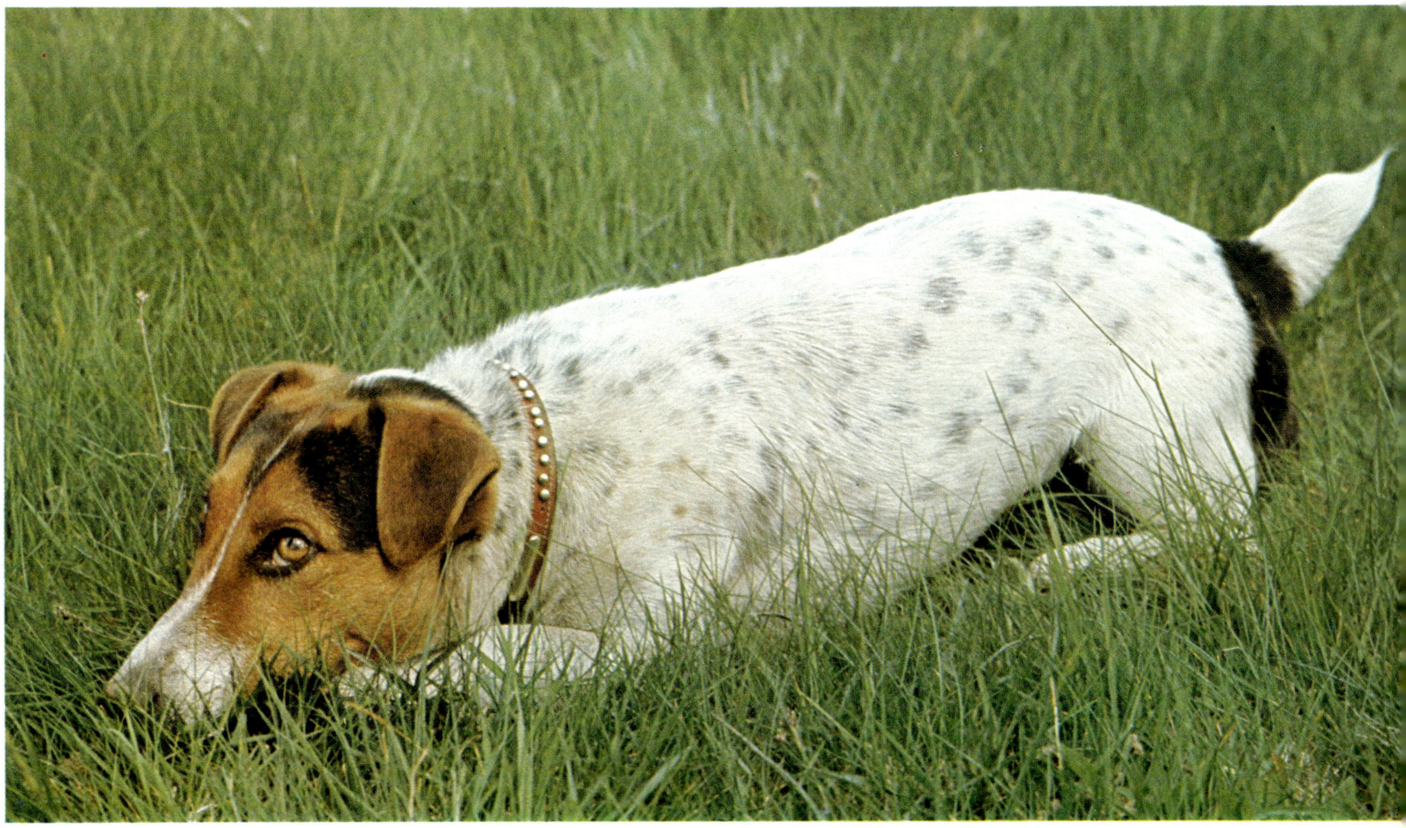

Left: The Cairn Terrier originated from the Isle of Skye, just off the west coast of Scotland. Originally, he was used to kill vermin, such as rats and wild cats. He is a delightful little dog, with an attractive shaggy coat.
Below left: The Jack Russell Terrier makes a lively family dog and companion.
Right: Fox Terriers are lively and friendly dogs, formerly used to attack vermin such as rats, rabbits and foxes. The Fox Terrier, which can be wire-haired or smooth-coated, was used to run with the hounds and came into his own when the fox went to earth.

has keen senses of smell and hearing. The dog's movements were slow and sure and very silent, and the gentleman with the fowling piece was led directly to the game.

As weapons become faster and more sophisticated, a more intelligent dog was needed and this arrived in the form of a Setter.

Dogs used in sport and hunting can be classified into several groupings, depending on what they do. For convenience the groupings used are the Gun Dogs, the Terriers, and other sporting dogs, including the Hounds.

**Gun Dogs**
These are dogs which hunt, point and retrieve birds from land or in water.
*English Setter*. This handsome and old-established setting dog is popular both in the USA and in Britain. He makes an attractive dog, with a coat either black-and-white, lemon-and-white or tricolour – black, white and tan. Dogs without heavy patches of colour, but flecked all over, are preferred.

As a show dog he has few equals and in temperament he is reliable, kind and intelligent.

*Gordon Setter*. This fine dog was first heard of at Gordon Castle, Banffshire in Scotland, and although many of these dogs have gone abroad, interest has revived in them since 1927 when the Gordon Setter Club was founded.

He is a stylish dog, built on galloping lines, with a coat of a deep shining coal-black, with tan markings of a rich chestnut.
*Irish Setter*. This is probably the best known setter in the world and possibly one of the oldest British Setters. He is sometimes referred to as the Red Setter because of his rich chestnut coloured coat, which must not bear any trace of black.

The Setter is a dog which delights in a good gallop and must be given a fair amount of exercise.
*Pointer*. This handsome and clean-cut gun dog is known the world over, with a fine, short, hard coat coloured lemon-and-white, orange-and-white, liver-and-white and black-and-white. He derives his name because he stands with head and tail stretched out when he scents game birds. This breed was known in Spain well over 200 years ago.
*Curly-coated Retriever*. Not often seen these days, he is a strong, smart and upstanding dog. He is one of the

oldest of British gun-dogs, with a highly distinctive coat formed of a mass of short, crisp curls, coloured black or liver. An excellent dog for retrieving game from water and a splendid companion and work dog.

*Flat-coated Retriever.* This dog originated from a cross between the Lesser Newfoundland and the Labrador Retriever. They were then crossed with Setters and Pointers and by 1860 a dog similar to the Flat-coated Retriever had been produced. He is superb with children, with a natural warmth that will endure anything from them. His colour is black or liver, with a fine textured coat as dense and flat as possible.

*Golden Retriever.* He is one of the greatest hunting dogs, with all the abilities of the Retriever and Setter, together with the scenting ability of the Bloodhound. He is most handsome, with a coat of an alluring golden colour. There are few better dogs for a home full of children as he is loyal and trustworthy.

*Labrador Retriever.* Contrary to popular belief this dog comes from Newfoundland, not Labrador. His ancestors are not quite clear and it is thought that they were first brought to Britain about 1800. At that stage they were crossed with the Flat-coated and the Curly-coated Retrievers to produce the Labrador we know today. He is an extremely friendly dog, with not a hint of aggression and for this reason he is ideal with children.

*Brittany Spaniel.* This attractive dog is well known in the USA, being among the twenty most popular breeds. It was not until 1975 that this breed was introduced into Britain. He is highly valued for his ability to hunt, and is famed for his pointing. They make excellent pets as well as being admirable working dogs. They are lightly built with a dense coat, usually in orange and white.

Left: Of all the Terrier breeds, the Bedlington Terrier is perhaps the oldest. He is a dog full of character, and has been known as the Gypsy Dog. He is a graceful and muscular fellow, with a springy gait. His head is pear-shaped, giving a lamb-like appearance. Right. The Australian Terrier was first shown in Melbourne, Australia, in 1885, and is one of the smallest working terriers. He is agile and very compact, and enjoys popularity in his own country, as well as Britain and the USA.

Above: It is essential that a Retriever is able to pick up a bird in its mouth without damaging it. This Golden Retriever is able to gently hold the duck and carry it direct to the sportsman. Dogs which are able to hold the game tenderly are said to have a 'soft' mouth.
Right: The Chesapeake Bay Retriever is an American breed which has never achieved the popularity its reputation might suggest. It is one of a number of breeds whose speciality is retrieving wildfowl from water, especially wild duck. One of the remarkable features of the breed is the coarse, oily coat which helps it shed water and ice simply by a good shake.

Left: The English Setter is exceptionally attractive as well as being a good working dog. He is extensively kept in America.

*Clumber Spaniel.* This dog took his name from Clumber, the seat of the Duke of Newcastle in Nottingham, England, where the breed was known in 1790. The Duke very much liked the breed and was responsible for making it popular in England during the mid-19th century.

He tends to be a serious dog and is a splendid retriever. His coat is plain white with lemon markings.

*Cocker Spaniel.* He gets his name from his work in finding and flushing out woodcock, being especially useful in thick scrub inaccessible to other spaniels. He is ideal as a family pet. His colouring can be extremely varied, but in main colours no white is allowed, except on the chest.

*Field Spaniel.* This breed is said to have been bred primarily for field-work from Sussex and Cocker Spaniels. He is better as a family dog than in the field, where he is rather slow. He is especially good in the home as he does not have a 'doggy' smell, which most families find objectionable. In colour he can be black, liver, golden liver, mahogany red or roan; or any of these colours with tan. The coat is flat or slightly waved, but never curled.

*Irish Water Spaniel.* The ancestors of this dog may go back several thousand years, for he is mentioned in Persian manuscripts. It is uncertain as to how he travelled to Britain, but he turns up in Shakespeare's *Two Gentlemen of Verona*, where the Bard gives mention to him.

His coat is formed of dense, tight and crisp ringlets, free from wooliness. And the colour is a rich, dark liver, having a purplish tint or bloom.

*English Springer Spaniel.* This is the oldest of our sporting gun dogs, and is the taproot from which all of our sporting land spaniels except the Clumber Spaniel have evolved. His coat is close, straight and weather resistant, without being coarse.

*Welsh Springer Spaniel.* This is said to be the only Spaniel native to Wales and is descended from a race mentioned in the Ancient Laws of Wales codified by Hywel Dda, some 1000 years ago. He is a handsome, conscientious and affectionate dog, with a rich red-and-white coat, straight and flat, thick and silky. It should never be wiry, wavy or curly.

*Sussex Spaniel.* He is a strong, short-legged flusher of game, well adapted to thick hedgerows and woodland scrub. His coat is a rich golden liver, abundant and flat, with no tendency to curl.

*Weimaraner.* This alert and attractive dog originated in Germany and was initially used for tracking game, although later he was trained to point and retrieve, a task to which he readily adapted. The Weimaraner has proven himself to be such an alert dog that police forces now use him, and when entered for obedience tests he always performs admirably. He is well known throughout the USA, and his smooth coat of a metallic silvery-grey makes him frequently admired.

## Terriers

These types of dog owe their name to the Latin word for earth, *terra*, and they are used to ferret out underground animals. Initially they were developed for use on farms, although they are now chiefly kept as pets.

*Airedale Terrier.* The Airedale has been called the world's best terrier because of his many good attributes. He was bred in Yorkshire, England, in the 1870s and takes his name from the River Aire. It is said that they were specifically bred to keep down the large number of rats around Bradford, Bingley and Otley, and were locally known as Waterside Terriers and Working Terriers.

He is the largest of all the Terriers, with a bright and friendly disposition. And he is good with children.

*Australian Terrier.* This is the smallest of the terriers, with a height at its shoulder of only 250 mm (10 in). His ancestry goes back to 1885, when he was first shown in a dog show in Melbourne, Australia.

He makes an excellent lively and spirited pet for a small house or flat.

*Bedlington Terrier.* This terrier inhabited the borders of England and Scotland during the early part of the last century, where he was used for otter and badger hunting. He is a graceful, lithe, muscular dog, with no sign of weakness. His head tends to be pear-shaped, with a mild and gentle expression. But when roused the dog's eyes sparkle, showing great courage and liveliness.

*Border Terrier.* He takes his name from the district around the English and Scottish border and is thought to be associated with the Dandie Dinmont and Bedlington breeds. He is very active and fond of following horses.

*Bull Terrier.* This breed looks quite ferocious, but is really a most companionable dog and reliable with children. He gained a reputation for ferocity when used in illegal pit contests. It is said that in one such contest a bull terrier killed a thousand rats in one hundred minutes!

He is thought of as the gladiator of the dog world, and is strongly built with a keen determined expression. They make faithful and affectionate companions.

*Cairn Terrier.* This is one of the oldest British Terriers. He is a smart and lively dog of a true terrier type, originating from the Isle of Skye.

Delightful in character, he has a compact body. His coat may be red, sandy, grey, brindled or nearly black.

*Dandie Dinmont.* This is a terrier of Scottish breeding, which takes its name from a farmer in Sir Walter Scott's *Guy Mannering*. This breed was used for otter-hunting, unearthing foxes and hunting other vermin infesting the Highlands.

Left: The Curly-coated Retriever is now a relatively rare breed. One of his ancestors was the Water Spaniel, from whom he derives his ability to retrieve game from salt flats and marshes. He has always been known for his tender mouth and steady nature and has been used to retrieve game such as quail and duck in New Zealand and Australia.

Above: The Irish Water Spaniel is said to be a cross between the Southern Irish Water Spaniel and the Northern Irish Water Spaniel. He is a smart and strongly-built dog, combining great intelligence and endurance. He has been known as the clown of the Spaniel family, due to his smooth face and curly topknot. His coat has tight ringlets, with a natural oiliness. Left: The Whippet is the result of breeding for speed. The breed was created by working-men in the north of England for the sport of rabbit coursing. He is a graceful animal, especially when running, and a delightful pet for the home.

Above: Hounds make up the hunting scene, adding colour and noise to an otherwise idyllic and tranquil country lane.

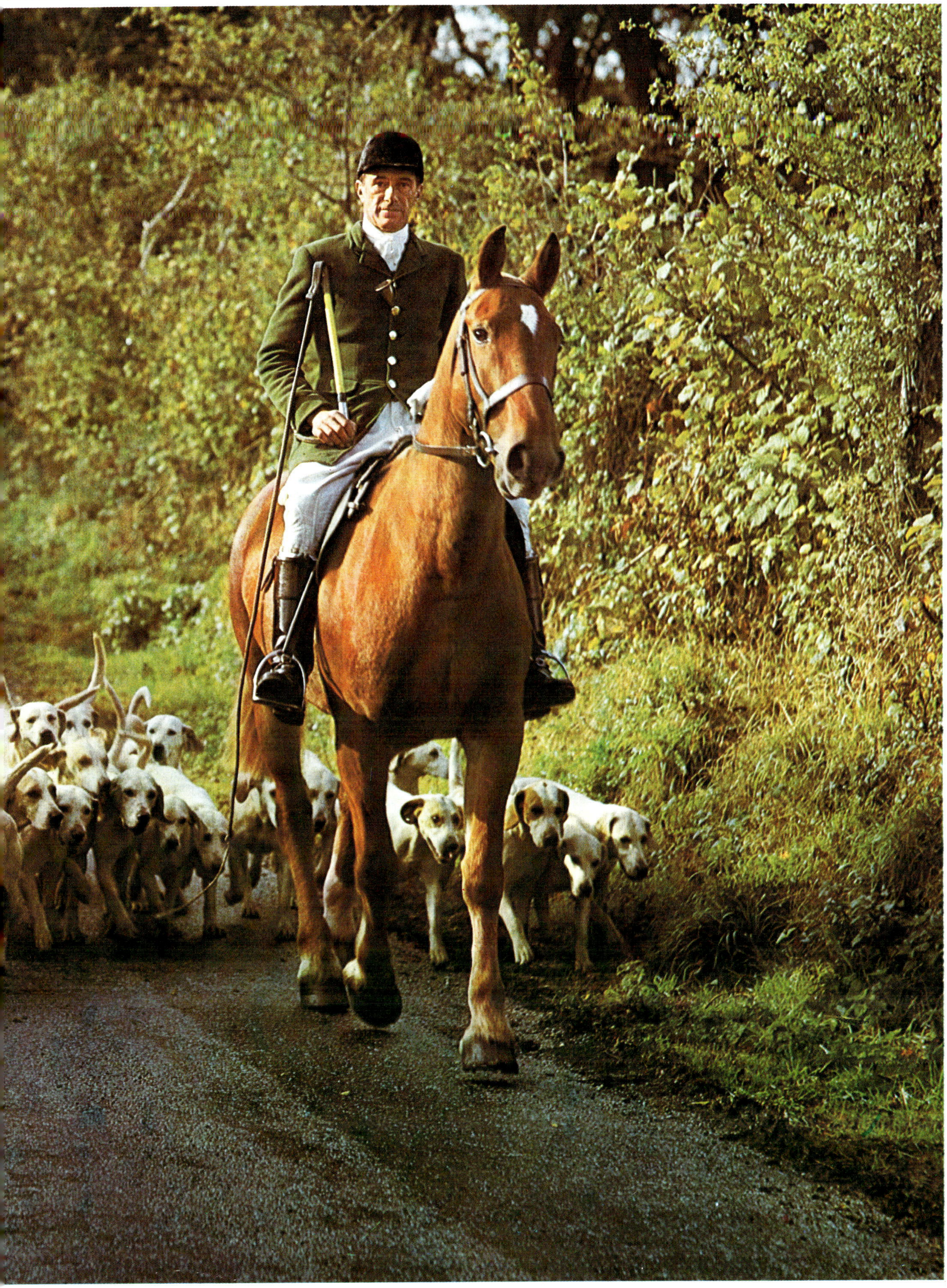

*Smooth Fox Terrier.* The general appearance of this delightful dog is one of liveliness. At one time he was the most popular of all the terriers. His early use was to bolt the fox which had gone to earth. He is most intelligent, extremely alert and very good as a pet.
*Wire Fox Terrier.* This is an older breed than the Smooth Fox Terrier and goes back to the mid-18th century. His coat is dense and wiry, but not curled.
*Irish Terrier.* Once he was one of the most widely-known terriers in Britain and was given the nickname 'Daredevil' because of his readiness to enter a fight with other dogs. His loyalty is unimpeachable and he is a lively, intelligent pet, excellent as a home guard.
*Kerry Blue Terrier.* This breed was taken up by breeders after World War I, before which it had been known as the Blue Irish. He was first known in the Irish mountain regions around County Kerry, from which he derives his name. He is a high spirited animal, even aggressive, with abundant energy and vigour. He makes a good house dog but does need to be taught self control when other dogs are around.
*Lakeland Terrier.* This terrier was previously known as the Cumberland and Westmorland Working Terrier and used to bolt foxes in the Lake District of England which had gone to earth. He is incredibly strong for his size and completely disregards danger.

Although he becomes devoted to one master, he does make a good family pet.
*Manchester Terrier.* Formerly known as the Black-and-tan Terrier he is an excellent ratter. He also makes a good pet. If you do not like a dog that barks a lot, then steer clear of this breed for they are sensitive to all sounds.

**Below: The Vizsla is a multi-purpose gun dog from Hungary which points game, marks the fall of the bird and then retrieves it on command.**

*Scottish Terrier.* This delightful and courageous terrier used to be called the Aberdeen Terrier until the rest of Scotland thought him good enough to be a national possession. His courage has earned him the title 'Die-hard'.

He's a dog with a will of his own, and often he tries to take over a family, imposing his own will.

*Sealyham.* This breed was specially developed in Pembrokeshire, South Wales, to tackle badgers. He makes an excellent loyal companion, but unless trained early tends to have a will of his own.

*Skye Terrier.* This breed is known to have existed in Skye and the Highlands for more than 300 years. He has a long coat, often some 125–150 mm (5–6 in) in length, which should be flat and firm and quite free from curls. He is thought to be one of the intelligentsia of the dog world and makes a devoted friend.

*Staffordshire Bull Terrier.* During the early 1800s the English Bulldog was crossed with the Old English Terrier to develop a dog for use in bull pits. Later, to perfect the breed, breeders crossed him with White English Terriers and Black-and-tan Terriers. When roused he can be very ferocious and for this reason it is not wise to select him as a family pet.

*Welsh Terrier.* A plucky working dog and a certain vermin killer, he owes much of his parentage to the rough-haired Black-and-tan Terriers.

Although often used as a hunting dog, he makes an excellent family pet and is especially affectionate and good with children.

*West Highland White Terrier.* This is a most delightful and enchanting short-legged terrier. His ancestors are

Below: The Weimaraner is a distinctive animal, originating in Germany. He is well known in the USA, where he is used as a gun dog. This striking dog also has a following in Britain.

**Right:** A group of Otter Hounds trailing along a river bank. **Far right:** The Basset Hound originated in France. He is a large dog with short legs, and therefore often gives the deceptive appearance of being small. He is used to hunt hares, with the followers on foot. Basset Hounds are famed for their ability to follow a scent, and have even been used to scent out truffles.

thought to be the Scottie, the Cairn and the Dandie Dinmont. He makes a good pet, although he tends to be a one-man dog.

## The Hound Breeds

These are dogs specializing as hunters of animals and can generally be divided into two groups. First there are the ones with long legs who detect their prey by sight. Second, there are the ones with short legs, who are slow and hunt by following a scent.

*Afghan Hound.* The Afghan Hound is a dignified and aloof creature, whose ancestors can be traced back 5000 or 6000 years when he was accepted among Egyptian royalty. Originally he was developed and trained for hunting in hilly regions.

Besides being an excellent hunter he makes a good family pet. He has the advantage of seldom barking and is never vicious.

He is so distinctive that everywhere he goes he is noticed, his head and tail held high and walking with a springy gait. At shoulder height he is some 685–735 mm (27–29 in) high.

*Basenji.* The Basenji, also known as the Congo Bush Dog and the Belgian Congo Dog, does not bark, but utters something more akin to a squeal or soft growl. Despite this, he makes a good house dog as he is alert and watchful. Basenjis were used by natives of the old Belgian Congo and southern Sudan for hunting wounded game, as they have exceptionally keen noses and are very fast.

Their ancestors can be traced back about three thousand years, when they were depicted on rock drawings.

*Basset Hound.* Most people today know what a Basset Hound looks like from the famous cartoon series featuring this breed. He is made to look quite human, with a superior appearance and don't-bother-me expression. He has also come to be popular through his good natured disposition with children, as it is almost impossible to annoy him.

*Beagle.* This hound is said to be a native of Britain. His coat may be rough or smooth and he is stockily built. The smallest of the British hounds, he is used extensively for hunting in packs.

*Bloodhound.* The history of this breed goes back a very long way. He is said to have been brought to Britain by the Normans. At that time he was a big black hound. The modern breed is thought to be the result of cross-breeding several different strains – the St Hubert, the Talbot and an old southern hound.

Aficionados of public houses will probably have noticed that many have signs depicting a pack of hounds. Often these hounds are known as Talbots.

This dog's great ability to track felons, and even apprehend miscreants individually amid large crowds, made him very useful to the gentry of the land. Indeed, it is because the dog was kept by the aristocracy that he got the name Bloodhound.

*Borzoi.* This breed is otherwise known as the Russian Wolfhound, because they were kept for hunting purposes and other sporting activities by the Russian tsars. They are very beautiful and graceful dogs, well noted for their bravery and speed.

As a pet he needs a great deal of attention and is generally very docile, but if annoyed he can bite with tremendous speed.

*Dachshund.* The term Dachshund in German means 'badger dog' and it was during the seventeenth century that a dog similar to the one we know today came to the attention of hunters. The dog's speciality

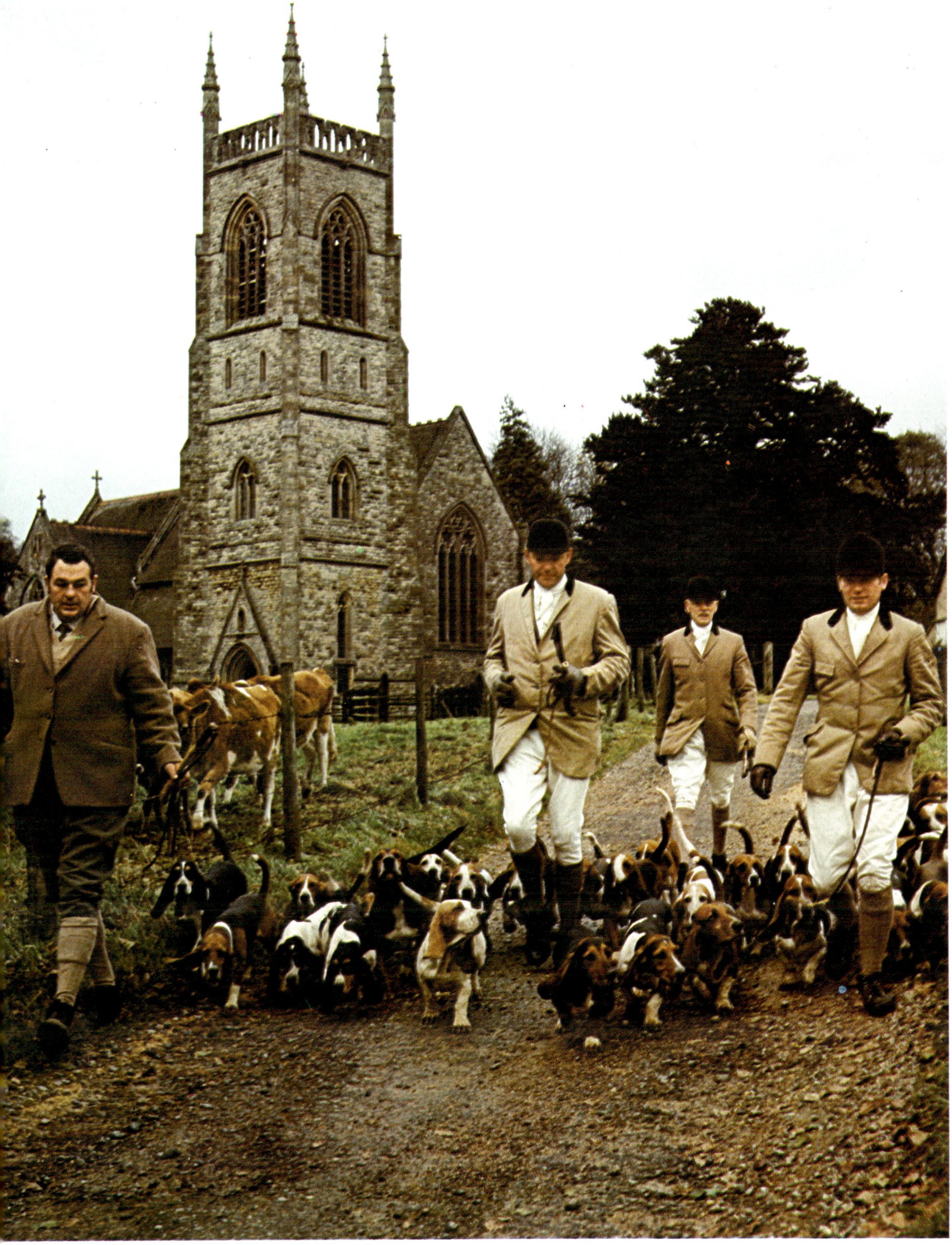

is pursuing badgers down holes, but he was also used against foxes and wounded deer. They make wonderful pets, being highly intelligent and very playful.

There are three types of dachshund: the Long-haired Dachshund, the Smooth-coated Dachshund and the Wire-coated Dachshund.

The Long-haired type has a soft and straight or slightly waved coat, of a shining colour. The coat tends to be longer under the neck and underparts of the body.

The Smooth-coated type should be long and low, with a short, dense, smooth and strong coat.

The Wire-coated type, with the exception of its jaw, eyebrows and ears, has a body completely covered with a short and even coat.

*Deerhound.* Doubtless this is one of the ancient dogs of Britain and he was formerly used for hunting deer in the Scottish Highlands. This earned him the titles Scottish Deerhound and the Royal Dog of Scotland. The breed goes back to the sixteenth century, when it was a favourite among Scottish chieftains. Such value was then put on the dogs that a brace of them could ransom a nobleman.

*Elkhound.* This powerful and distinctive dog hails from Norway where his ancestors were used 4000 years ago to herd flocks and defend villagers from wolves. These dogs have a will of their own and anyone thinking of owning one should be competent to train dogs.

*Finnish Spitz.* Finland has provided us with one of the most beautiful of dogs. The large family of Spitz is one of the oldest to have been domesticated. The first Finnish Spitz was brought to England in 1927 and since then this has become an established breed. They make excellent family dogs.

*Greyhound.* This breed is famed for being the fastest dog in the world. Its history goes back 4000 years in Egyptian history. He is also recorded in the Laws of Canute, enacted in 1016 AD. Perhaps he is best known today for his turn of speed at greyhound tracks, where several dogs at a time are trained to chase a mechanical hare for the financial profit or loss of spectators, as well as for their entertainment.

These are reserved, cautious and highly strung animals and do not often make good family pets.

*Irish Wolfhound.* This is the tallest and probably most powerful of dogs and is said to claim descent from the courts of ancient Irish kings. A dog of this breed can weigh 54 kg (120 lb) and stand 775 mm (31 in) high at the shoulder. It is a striking hound in appearance.

*Rhodesian Ridgeback.* This is a breed also known as the African Lion Hound or the Rhodesian Lion-dog. Its peculiarity is a ridge on its back, formed by the hair growing in the opposite direction to the rest of the coat. This ridge is clearly defined and symmetrical, starting behind the shoulders and continuing to the hip bones. The width of the ridge of hairs is about 50 mm (2 in).

The origin of this breed goes back many hundreds of years to when German, Dutch and French Huguenots emigrated to South Africa. The dogs they took with them mated with half-wild native dogs, producing the ancestors of the dog we know today. He is certainly a one-man dog and makes an excellent guard dog.

*Saluki.* Often known as the Gazelle Hound, the Saluki is thought to be the Royal Dog of Egypt and is said to have been a distinct breed and type of dog 300 years BC, but he is much older than that. His coat is smooth and silky and coloured white, cream, fawn, golden, red or grizzle. He can also be black-and-tan-and-white or black-and-tan.

*Whippet.* This breed is a miniature English greyhound, and is often thought of as the working man's greyhound. He is the fastest dog for his weight in the world, capable of speeds up to 56 km/hr (35 miles/hr).

These attractive animals were used by miners as rabbiting dogs, which were later trained to run a 183 m (200 yd) course. Dogs frequently covered this distance in twelve seconds.

**Left:** The Norwegian Elkhound is a dog exhibiting great stamina, and has been used to guard both the home and flocks of sheep. **Below:** The Irish Wolfhound is the largest of the Hound group. He is a noble dog, whose ancestors are mentioned in early Irish literature, when they were greatly prized.

# Working with man

Through the centuries dogs have been used in many ways in the service of man. A dog's ability to be trained to act on the word of command or at the sound of a whistle have been exploited to man's advantage.

This ability, coupled with the dog's inbred aggression and his defence mechanisms have made him ideal as a guard dog. Indeed, at one time dogs were used in war. Suits of armour worn by dogs can be seen in many museums in European countries.

The oldest breed in Britain used as a dog of war was the Mastiff, a large and very strong dog with incredible strength.

These dogs so impressed the Romans that when they invaded Britain many were taken back to Rome to fight in arenas against bears, bulls and lions. This noble breed of dog had outstanding courage; at the beginning of the nineteenth century, Sydenham Edwards wrote in *Cynographia Britannica*, 'What the lion is to the cat, the Mastiff is to the dog'. These dogs were used many centuries ago to protect castles and farms from marauding packs of wolves.

Today, guard dogs take many forms, often depending on what is required of them. The small, black, cobby, tailless Schipperke has been used to guard barges in Belgium. He is a dog with a distinctive sense of his master's property.

Perhaps the most widely known breeds used today as guard dogs are German Shepherd Dogs, often called Alsatians, and Dobermann Pinschers. Despite this common role, they can be reared as family pets, especially if taken into the home when young. But the Dobermann Pinscher will need firm handling and discipline.

The characteristic expression of the Alsatian is one of perpetual vigilance, alertness and watchfulness. The Dobermann Pinscher is also bold and alert, with a sleek build that gives a fast and 'elastic' gait. This breed was specially developed for the purpose of being a good police and guard dog by the German Louis Dobermann in the 1870s. He crossed a number of local breeds to get the type of dog he wanted.

Many other breeds have been used as guards, including Great Danes, Boxers and the Lhasa Apso, which is usually associated with monasteries in Tibet. This is an attractive dog that needs plenty of grooming.

The Keeshond was used in Holland at the beginning of the nineteenth century to guard farms and barges. He is a medium sized dog with a happy and sensible disposition.

### Dogs for the Blind

The great humanitarian work in training dogs to act as guides to blind people originated in Europe. It was after World War I that blinded German soldiers were given trained guide dogs. This was sponsored by the Government. The scheme was so successful that other countries soon adopted the idea. The pioneers in this development were Switzerland, France and Italy.

Today, the scheme is world-wide and in America use is made of breeds such as Dobermann Pinschers, Boxers and Alsatians.

In Britain, many breeds have been used and the most satisfactory have been Labradors, Alsatians and Retrievers.

Mostly bitches which have been spayed are used, as they are less likely to be distracted by other dogs. But castrated dogs have been used quite successfully.

The training of a guide dog takes about four months and the prospective owner undertakes a training session lasting three to four weeks. It is absolutely essential that on leaving the training establishment both the dog and its owner are in harmony and have complete trust in one another.

### Police Dogs

Most of the police forces have come to acknowledge the use of dogs in police work, not just for adding weight to their ranks, but for essential and specialized jobs such as tracking, scenting drugs and explosives, rescue work and apprehending criminals.

The most successful breed for this work has been Alsatians, but increasingly Dobermann Pinschers are

**Right: The versatile Border Collies have been selected for their working abilities for many generations.**

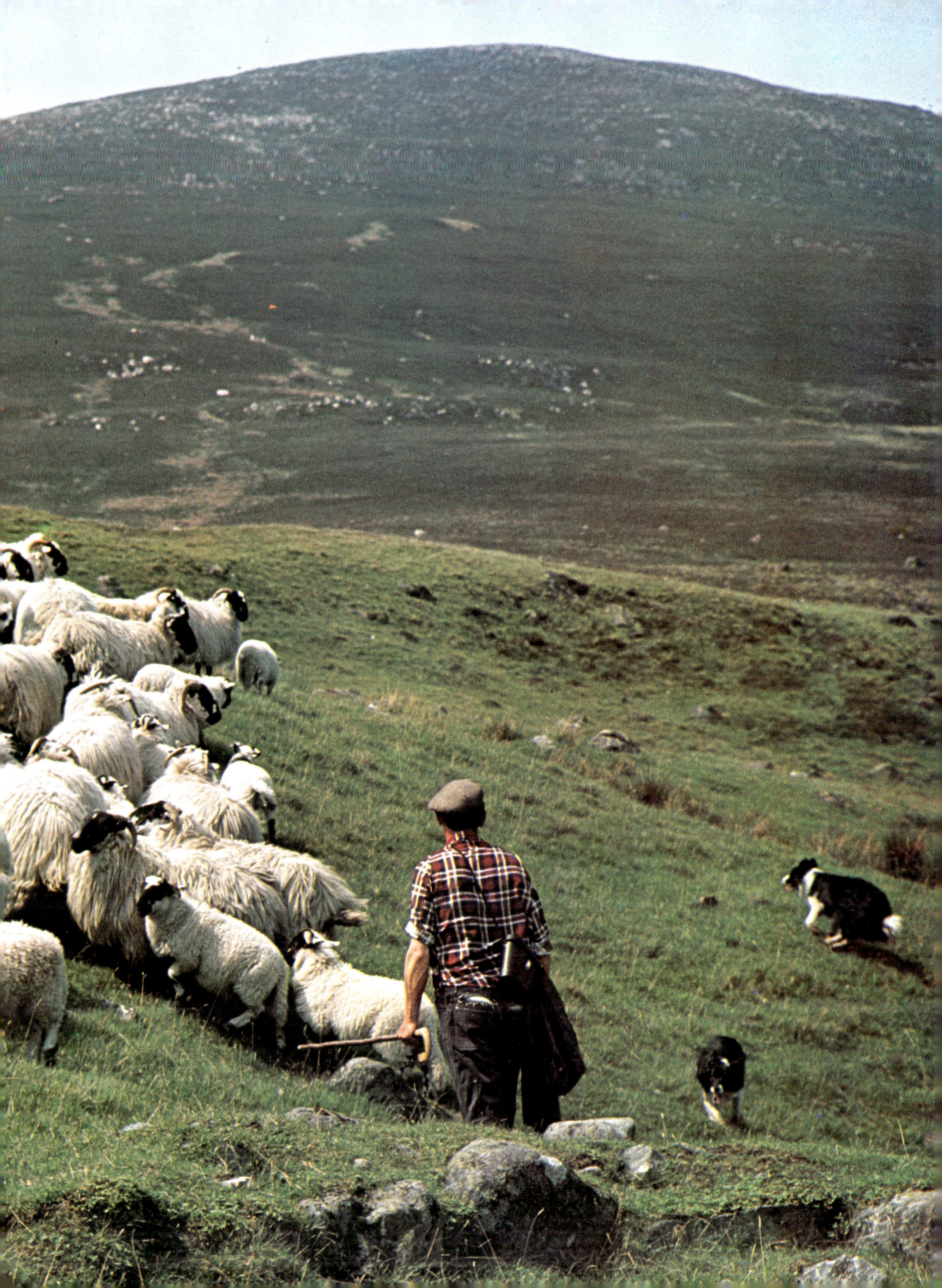

being used in Germany and America. Labradors have shown their capability in detecting drugs, and are often used by police in dock areas and airports.

**Pastoral Dogs**
The Englishman's idea of a sheepdog is the Collie or the Old English Sheepdog, which often appears to be more like a bale of tasselled hay on four hairy legs!

The range of herding dogs throughout the world is wide, to suit greatly differing climates and terrains. Some not only act as shepherds of animals, but as guard dogs as well. For instance, the Russian Owtcharka, which may have to deal with wolves and other marauding animals, can be 800 mm (32 in) at the shoulder, whereas an English pastoral animal such as the Shetland Sheepdog may be only 300 mm (12 in). The Owtcharka, often known as the Russian Sheepdog, is seldom seen outside of Russia. Although most Russian sheep-herding dogs resemble the Spitz type, the Owtcharka bears more resemblance to the Old English Sheepdog. Another dog well suited to cold climates is the Komondor, one of the largest cattle and sheep herding dogs but primarily a guard dog. It is one of the oldest national races of dogs and is thought to be over 1000 years old, dating back to the great Magyar migration.

It is a dog with a quite extraordinary coat, which resembles an impenetrable coat of tangled knots and cords, but which protects it against all weathers. The breed is a giant among dogs.

The Old English Sheepdog's ancestry can only be traced back about two centuries, so it is a puzzle to know where the term *Old* came from. Often he is called the Bobtailed Sheepdog, due to the custom of docking the tail.

Probably the best known of all sheepdogs is the Collie. This name is taken from the old title of Colley Dog, which was given to the breed many years ago and probably derived from a breed of mountain sheep herded by Scottish farmers. In fact, the Colleys are ancestors of the famous highland sheep which have black feet and masks. Besides the well-known Rough-coated Collies, there are the Smooth-coated Collie and the Bearded Collie. The only difference between the rough-coated and the smooth-coated breeds is that the latter has a smooth outline, with a clean-cut appearance, whereas the Bearded Collie is quite different.

The Bearded Collie more resembles the Old English Sheepdog, which was probably one of its ancestors. It has had many names throughout its history, including the Mountain Collie, the Highland Collie and the Hairy Mou'ed Collie. It is a breed which was much on the decline a few years ago, but it has recently been refound. They are attractive and very good with children.

A well-known cattle-herding dog in the British Isles is the Welsh Corgi. There are two distinct breeds of Corgi, the Cardigan and the Pembroke. Of the two, the Cardigan is the elder and is said to have been brought to Wales about 1200 BC by the Central European Celts. Used to herd cattle, he was subsequently bred with native dogs and Dachshunds to produce the dog we know today. He is distinguished from the Pembroke type by having a long tail.

The Pembroke Corgi goes back to the twelfth century, when he was brought to Wales by Flemish weavers. At this stage he more resembled the Schipperke. Through subsequent crossing with the Cardigans the dog we know today was developed.

There are, of course, many other cattle herding dogs in the world. These include the Bouvier of Flanders, the Australian Heeler, the Hungarian Pumi and the Portuguese Cattle Dog.

The Australian Heeler, also known as the Australian Cattle Dog, is a relatively new breed, whose ancestors probably included the old blue-merle coloured Collie, the Kelpie and the Australian Wild Dog, the Dingo.

His coat is short, as one might expect for a dog in a

Above: The Pembroke Corgi can be a lovable little dog, although he has a tendency to be snappy and short tempered. Originally, he was used to herd cattle.
Above right: The Australian Cattle Dog is very agile and rugged. Indeed, he has to be to survive the tough conditions when rounding up and penning cattle over large distances in Australia. Right: The Komondor, a breed originating in Hungary, is one of the largest sheep and cattle-working dogs. He is frequently exhibited in the USA.

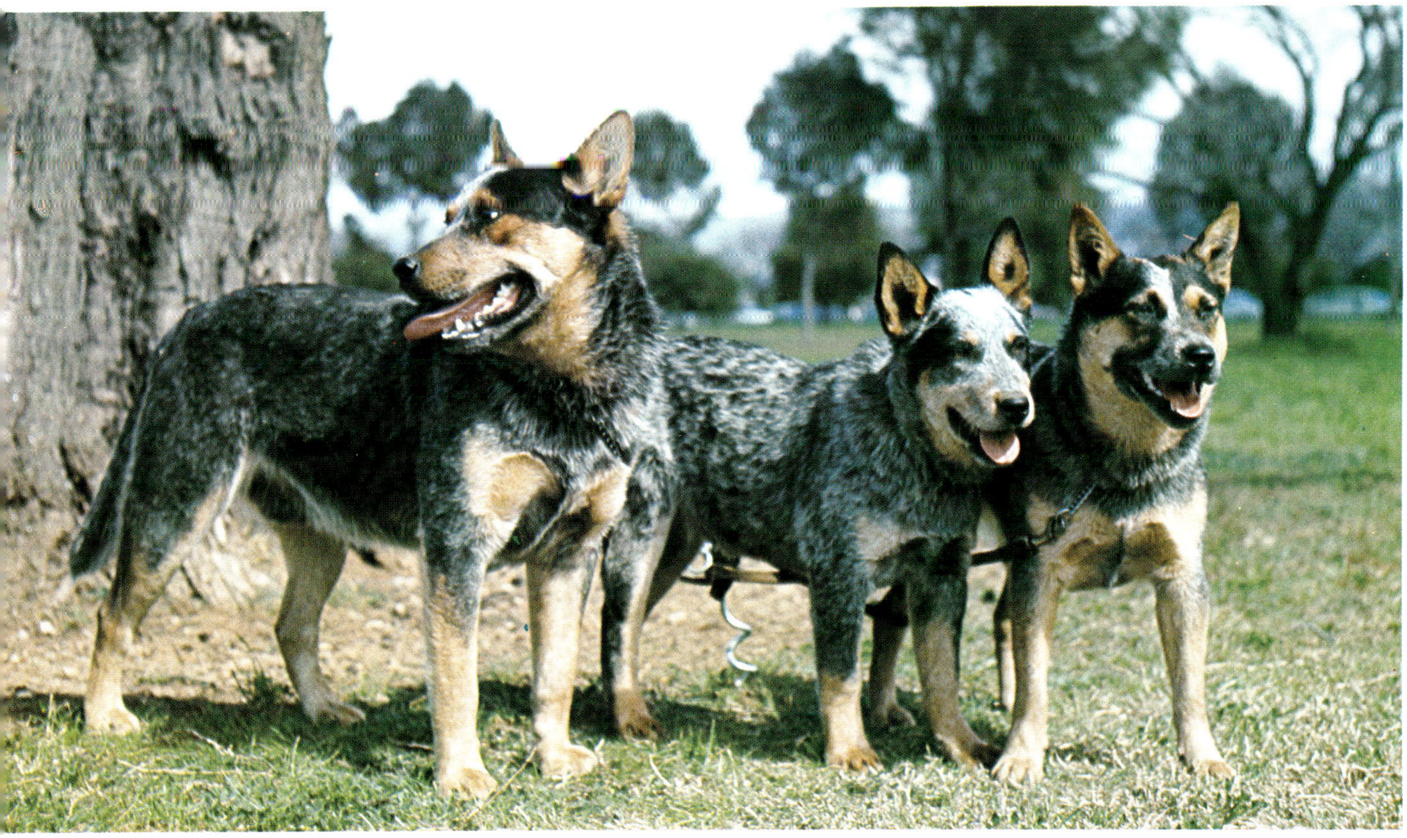
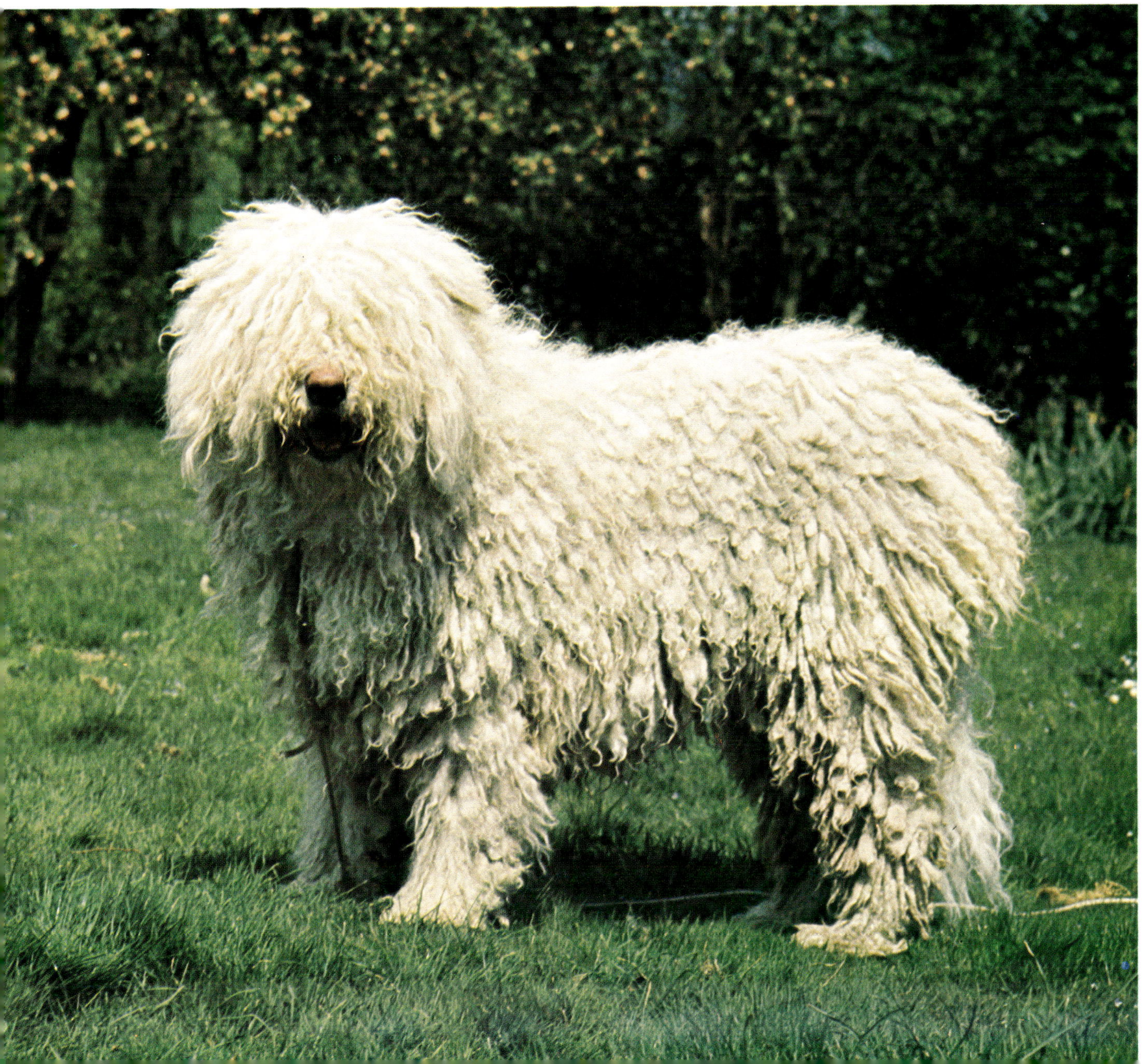

Above: Many polar explorers owe their lives to husky sled dogs, whose deep coats enable them to survive exceptionally cold conditions.

85

Left: Several different breeds of dogs have been used for guiding blind people. These include Labradors, Golden Retrievers, Alsatians and Boxers. It is essential, however, that the dog and the blind person are carefully matched to ensure that they are compatible. Spayed bitches are mostly used, but quite a number of castrated dogs are now successfully employed as guide dogs. The dog wears a harness, through which the blind person can be guided. Right: Dogs are used in different ways by police forces throughout the world. Recently, they have been introduced to help detect drugs hidden in cargoes. This Yellow Labrador is searching for cannabis.

warm country, and close. They are superbly adapted for rounding up and penning range cattle. Usually they are blue or mottled blue, but red-and-tan and red-and-white dogs are seen

## Draught Dogs

For many centuries dogs have been used to haul sledges or small carts in many parts of the world. Not so long ago large and strong dogs, such as Mastiffs, were used in continental Europe to pull carts.

At one time it is estimated that some 175,000 dogs were used in Belgium alone to pull carts for tradesmen such as bakers and grocers. Indeed, they were used in England but were banned from the streets of London in 1839 and from public highways in Britain in 1854. They made a thorough nuisance of themselves by incessant barking.

It may seem cruel to put dogs into the shafts of carts, but they were well protected by the municipal councils of the areas in which they worked. This is especially true in Switzerland and Belgium. The vehicles and harness were inspected thoroughly and regularly and many checks were made without prior notice. The weight of the loads was strictly limited: For a single dog the dead weight could not exceed 136 kg (300 lb) and for two dogs 181 kg (400 lb).

The animals were even protected by laws against their use in inclement weather, when some protection had to be given. In Italy there existed a law which provided that a dog of burden, or a guard dog, had to be supplied with a sunshade during the hottest part of the day!

## Hauling Sledges

Early polar exploration owes a great deal to the strength, fortitude and courage of huskies, overcoming the almost insuperable difficulties of those regions.

At first, sledge dogs were not so far removed from the parent wolf stock, when severe and often inhumane treatment was meted out to them. But by the time of the great polar exploration of Antarctica the dogs were better used and treated and improved results were achieved.

The term 'husky' means a sledge dog; but not all sledge dogs are huskies. Many authorities suggest that dogs below the 55th parallel have a preponderance of non-husky blood in them. North of the line the dogs improve in hardiness and likeness to the true husky.

The harnesses for the dogs has to be strong and comfortable, enabling them to haul sledges for long periods. Several types of hitches have been used, the traditional one being in the shape of a fan. Usually twelve to fifteen dogs are attached separately to the sledge by long traces, making it easy to see if all the dogs are pulling strongly. However, sometimes as few as seven and as many as eighteen are used.

A type of hitch more used is the double Indian file

hitch, where paired dogs are hitched one behind the other. This has the advantage in that all the pulling is in line with the sledge. In the fan hitch some of the lateral pulling is wasted. In the Indian file hitch the number of dogs is usually eight, although this can be as few as six and as many as sixteen.

**Hunting Truffles**

Perhaps one of the most unusual uses to which a dog has been put is to scent out truffles. These are small, leafless and rootless fungi, belonging to the family *Ascomycetes*. These fungi are relished by gourmets, especially in France; truffled turkey and other game stuffed with truffles being very popular.

These fungi grow between September and the end of February, slightly below the soil surface and usually in woods of beech and oak, although they are also to be found in woods of poplar, chestnut, hazel, elm, willow and lime.

In France, dogs of the Poodle type, called Truffleurs were used. These dogs weigh about 16 kg (35 lbs) and stand 430–460 mm (17–18 inches) high, with a shaggy coat. These dogs had to have an excellent sense of smell, and they could often detect the fungi at 100 yards distance if growing in light and fairly loose soil and not below 3 inches deep. The truffles give off their strongest scent when in prime condition, which lasts a few days before deterioration.

Below: The Dobermann Pinscher is often used as a police or army dog, especially in the United States of America. This breed was the creation of Louis Dobermann, a German who crossed a number of local breeds. Right: The Saint Bernard, the canine giant, is one of the ten most popular breeds in the United States of America. These dogs are associated with legendary feats of rescue, finding and guiding to safety travellers lost in the snow.

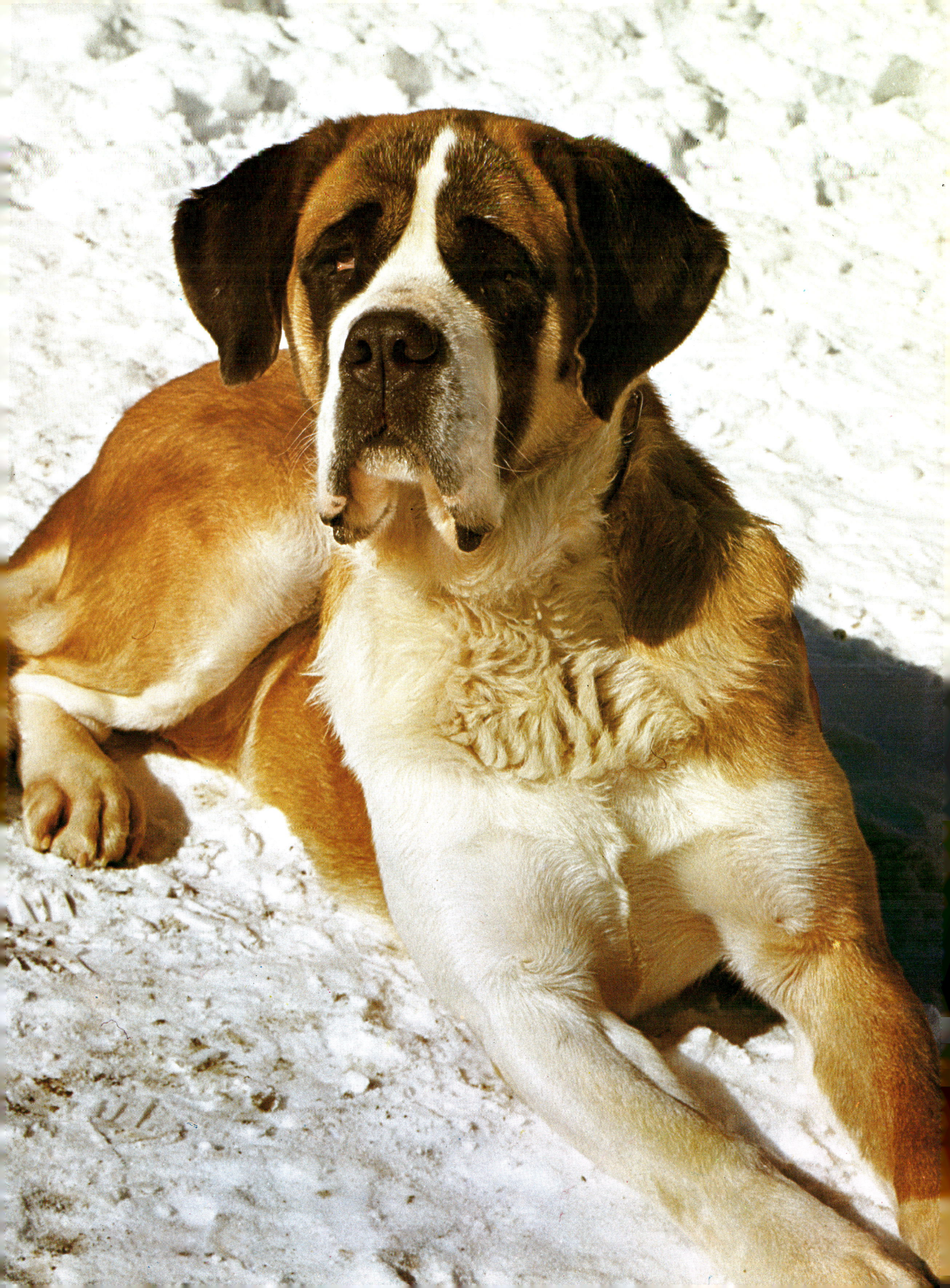

# Obedience training

A well behaved and obedient dog is a joy to watch and a delight to his master. Furthermore, he is a safe animal, taking discipline as a normal part of his life.

Dogs which have no road-drill sense, dashing after motor cars and bicyclists and constantly barking, are a misery to themselves, a shame to their owners and a certain hazard to road users. Many road accidents are caused each year by dogs leaping about roads, often in pursuit of a bitch.

Training a dog starts when he is a puppy, at a time when everything is new to him. At that stage the instructor is not correcting a dog already wayward and disobedient, but moulding a puppy into a creature with which it will be a pleasure to live.

## Training the Puppy

The first lessons a dog receives are the ones to housetrain him, and this has been explained in 'Choosing a puppy'. Do not attempt to do any other training until he is well and truly housetrained.

To confuse him with a further set of commands and exercises before he has mastered the first will cause confusion in his mind. In any case, obedience training does not usually start before the puppy is eight to fifteen months old.

*The principles of training.* These are quite simple and straightforward. Dogs do not learn by reasoning out problems, but simply by association of ideas and rewards for doing something right or wrong. That is to say, if a dog does something right and you reward him with a smile, a pat on the head and 'Well done, boy', he will do the same thing correctly again.

Dogs are eager to please and delighted to find a human master. However, dogs do vary in their submissiveness to a master. Strong willed dogs require strong willed owners. This is not to say that it is necessary to beat a dominant dog, you should just take a firm line with him.

Most dog owners are not interested in advanced dog handling. All they require is for the dog to come to them when called, to sit and to lie down, and to walk on a lead and have street manners.

Praise and punishment should be given at the time of doing the deed, not hours later. It is almost impossible to over-praise the dog – he will wallow in however much praise he gets.

Similarly, any admonishment should be given straightaway. A stern face and a 'Bad boy' will quickly teach him that he has been naughty. To wait until you arrive home and then to hit him will only make him think that he is being smacked for coming home.

*Teaching the puppy his name.* As dogs learn by association of ideas, the quickest and easiest way of teaching a puppy his name is to associate it with food as the reward. As you put his food down, call him quite clearly and distinctly, so that as he arrives you are putting his dish down.

In his mind this means that when he answers to his name he will be rewarded by food. It is quite surprising how quickly he will get to understand.

*Starting training.* Take the puppy to a quiet part of the garden where it is enclosed at the back and sides of him. Walk a few paces away and call him by name. If he does not come at once, extend a hand to him. He will gambol to you. At this stage reward him with praise and a titbit of food. He should then be made to sit down.

When he has eaten his morsel of food repeat this all over again. It is essential to have him come to you easily before taking him outside of your garden and to the local park. If he will not come to you in his own garden, with no distractions, he certainly will not come to you in a park with other dogs and children playing around him.

Don't move the training out of your garden until he comes when called and sits. These simple acts establish a basis for further training and give the basics of discipline.

*Lead training.* The way to accustom the puppy to a lead has been explained in 'Caring for your pet', and it is as well to have the puppy thoroughly used to wearing a collar by the time you are training him. It then becomes easy, once you have him coming to you

**Right:** This well-mannered little Cairn Terrier is making his request in the politest possible way. Most dogs learn to beg without any difficulty.

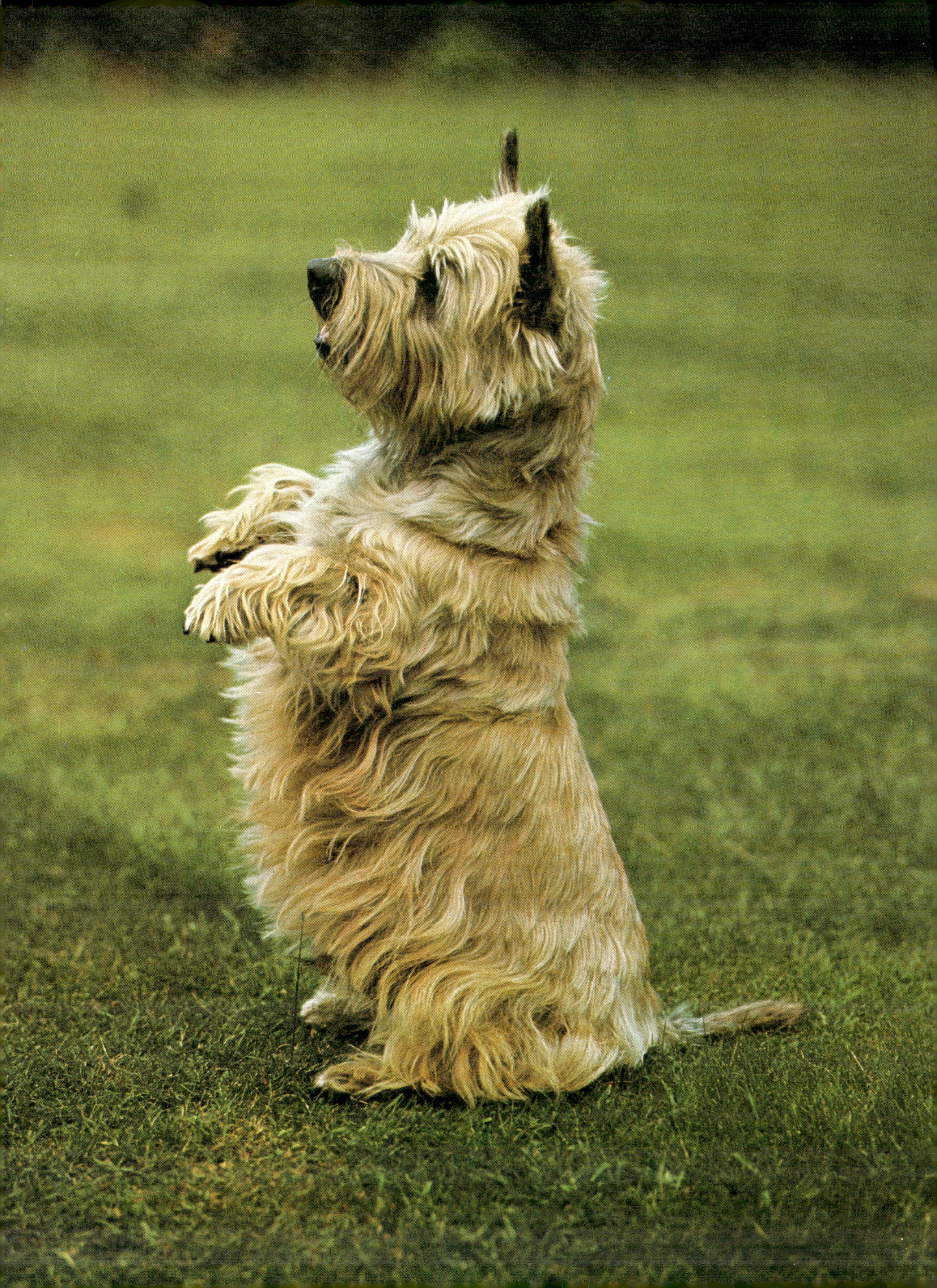

and sitting, to fix a lead on to the collar. This is a major milestone in his training, for through a natural process which the dog can understand you now have him on the end of a lead, sitting down and ready to move off at your command.

The question will arise about the type of collar to have. Basically, there are two – the buckled collar and the slip chain collar. Of the two the chain collar is by far the more comfortable when not in use and attached to a lead. With the chain type it is easier to correct the dog, when he does wrong, by pulling the lead. This may sound slightly cruel, but when it is accompanied by a 'Bad boy' in a sharp voice the dog soon gets the message. But temper the vigour of the pull according to the size of the animal. A tug given to a Whippet may not even be felt by an Irish Wolfhound!

When the puppy is on a lead with a slip collar, the next step is to associate the commencement of walking with one word, and I suggest this should be 'Walk'.

It is almost certain that during the first time out on a lead he will pull and try to free himself; this is only to be expected. He will soon find that there is no escape, and the sooner he realizes this the better. When he does accept the lead and walk correctly, praise him lavishly.

**Above:** Dogs can be taught to respond to whistle signals. This Labrador Retriever knows a raised hand means sit, and is now being made to act on one short pip of a whistle. **Right:** If you have been unable to make your dog respond to his name, it is worth resorting to the extreme measure of tying a long cord to his collar. Allow him to walk away, then call his name. If he does not respond, give the lead a jerk.

It is as well to associate the lead and collar with the excitement of going for walks. There is then a greater chance that he will easily accept the lead and collar. Even if you are taking him a few yards to the local park, take him on a lead so that he associates the lead and collar with going to have fun.

The eventual aim is to have the dog walking on your left side, with the lead in your right hand.

The length of time it takes to train a young dog to walk beside you on a lead varies considerably; some dogs learn in a fortnight, others take longer. Chocolate drops and other tasty morsels can be used as rewards. Take care not to make each lesson too long and tire him.

When he pulls on the lead, pull it back sharply and say 'Heel', so that he associates this word with walking alongside you on a lead.

A traumatic time for him will be when you first take

him out into the street and he is aware of motor cars and people. He may be wary of them and require reassurance that you are there.

At some time when he is out he will most certainly want to relieve himself. He should be discouraged from doing this on the pavement and therefore nudge him towards the gutter. He should be made to understand that all calls of nature must be in the gutter.

*Kerb drill.* Crossing a road is another big step in his life. Always make him sit at the kerb, saying 'Sit'. Reward him with a pat and 'Good boy'.

For safety, it is essential that he does sit at the kerb. It then gives you a chance to check on the traffic and to select a good time to cross. When you are ready to cross, say 'Walk' to him and walk confidently over the road.

Let him realize that you are in control and know what you are doing. Dithering at the kerb will only serve to make both of you unsure and frightened.

This walking by your side is usually known as 'walking to heel', and can be either on the lead or walking free by the side of you. Of course this is part of advanced training. And indeed as soon as he is able to do that he can then be made to sit, even when not on a lead.

## Training Classes

During recent years owners have become more aware of the need to train their dogs. In response to this, many dog obedience classes have been started. These classes are of enormous value, providing professional help for both the owner and the dog.

They usually like the dog to be at least six months old and the puppy should be able to walk on the lead, but this is not always essential.

The cost of these classes is not high and they are certainly worth the time devoted to them. They are usually good fun for both the owner and dog. But do not treat them as reform centres for recalcitrant animals as they really are schools under the guidance of an experienced dog handler.

As your dog is in close proximity to other dogs at these schools, it is an ideal time to teach him not to pay any attention to other dogs.

If you have a family it is a good idea to get one of your older children to take the dog at the obedience classes. This helps to form a good relationship between the dog and youngster and will give your son or daughter the opportunity to learn something of community spirit.

## Obedience Tests

Most dogs like to show off their competence and training and ability to perform obedience tests. Obedience tests and working trials are often held at dog shows, particularly those situated in the country, and they are great fun. The dogs are judged and scored solely on how they perform the tests.

Competitions are held in most countries, and quite naturally the rules and regulations and what is expected of the dog varies from one country to another.

Therefore, it is essential first to visit the tests as a spectator before entering with your own dog. You will be able to get a feel of the competition and know exactly what is expected of both you and your dog. Also obtain a copy of the rules and regulations governing the tests, and study them carefully.

However, remember that if you are a newcomer to these tests it is not wise to be too ambitious at the start. Select an easy class and do well in it; this is far better than doing rather poorly in a much higher and more difficult class.

Although there are often many different classes, usually it is only the novice section that is of any interest. Most people just want to demonstrate their dog's ability to do the basic obedience tests. In both

Above: The Basenji is a very old hunting dog and was well known in ancient Egypt. He is lightly built, having gazelle-like grace. Right: The Large Munsterlander, a German sporting breed, was decimated in the two World Wars but it is now becoming more common.

America and Britain there are novice classes. For example, the American novice class, as laid down by the American Kennel Club, requires the following test to be completed.

The first is a temperament test. The owner, with the dog on the lead, brings the dog to the stand position. The judge then approaches and rubs his hand gently over the dog's back. It is possible that the judge will talk to the dog to give it reassurance that all is well. However, any resentment to this treatment, such as growling or cringing, will be penalized. Secondly, the dog has to walk to heel on the lead. Thirdly, he has to walk to heel without the lead. Fourthly, the handler has to recall his pet from the sitting or down position, the dog having to approach and sit at heel. Fifthly, the dog must sit for one minute with the handler in sight. And finally, the dog has to adopt a down position for three minutes, again with the handler in sight.

In Britain, the tests for this class are basically the same, except that the down position is only necessary for two minutes. In addition, the dog has to recover a dumb-bell.

There are, of course, further classes which are much more difficult. The most difficult, for instance, is a test that involves the dog working at heel, sitting for two minutes with the handler out of sight, being sent away, dropping and being recalled, retrieving any article, adopting the down position for ten minutes with the handler out of sight, discriminating by scent, and control from a distance.

Most dogs, of course, never reach these advance standards, being quite happy to pass the novice test.

**Some Thoughts About The Handler**
Much can be said about training the dog, either for basic obedience training or for entering tests, and something also needs to be said about the handler. The dog can be trained to perform his part as if by clockwork, as long as the handler plays his part correctly.

Obviously, the best way to learn the theory and practice of dog handling is for both of you to attend a dog obedience training session where you can have professional advice.

The next best is for several people each with a dog to set up a school on their own. By training with other people and their dogs it is possible to simulate show conditions better than when on your own.

Apart from these classes, for road manners and obedience it is necessary to train the dog in conditions he would normally encounter. This is not to say that after one lesson you take him down to the high street on Saturday morning and perform your dog training repertoire outside the busiest supermarket. Both of you will probably be jostled and this will make the dog very wary about obeying future instructions.

It is necessary to be sensible about this and first to select a piece of open ground away from people and other dogs. Then gradually select busier places until on quiet days the high street can be tackled.

If you decide to enter a show, start off with the easiest class. Build up slowly both your own and your dog's confidence. Preparation for the show is important, but it must not be preceded by a sudden rush to cram in more training.

It takes a long time for the dog to have full confidence in his handler and this can be destroyed if an unprepared dog is rushed into a show above his ability.

Most first-attempt failures at shows are through the handler getting nervous, through not preparing himself thoroughly. The essential element when first taking part with your dog in an obedience test is to maintain a feeling of co-operation between the dog and yourself, so that he does not lose confidence in you. It does not matter what the judges think of you, so long as your dog thinks you're wonderful. Give him plenty of praise and affection when he has done something right.

All beginners start somewhere and if your dog steps out of his first competition feeling happy, then it is a good omen for his – and your – next attempt.

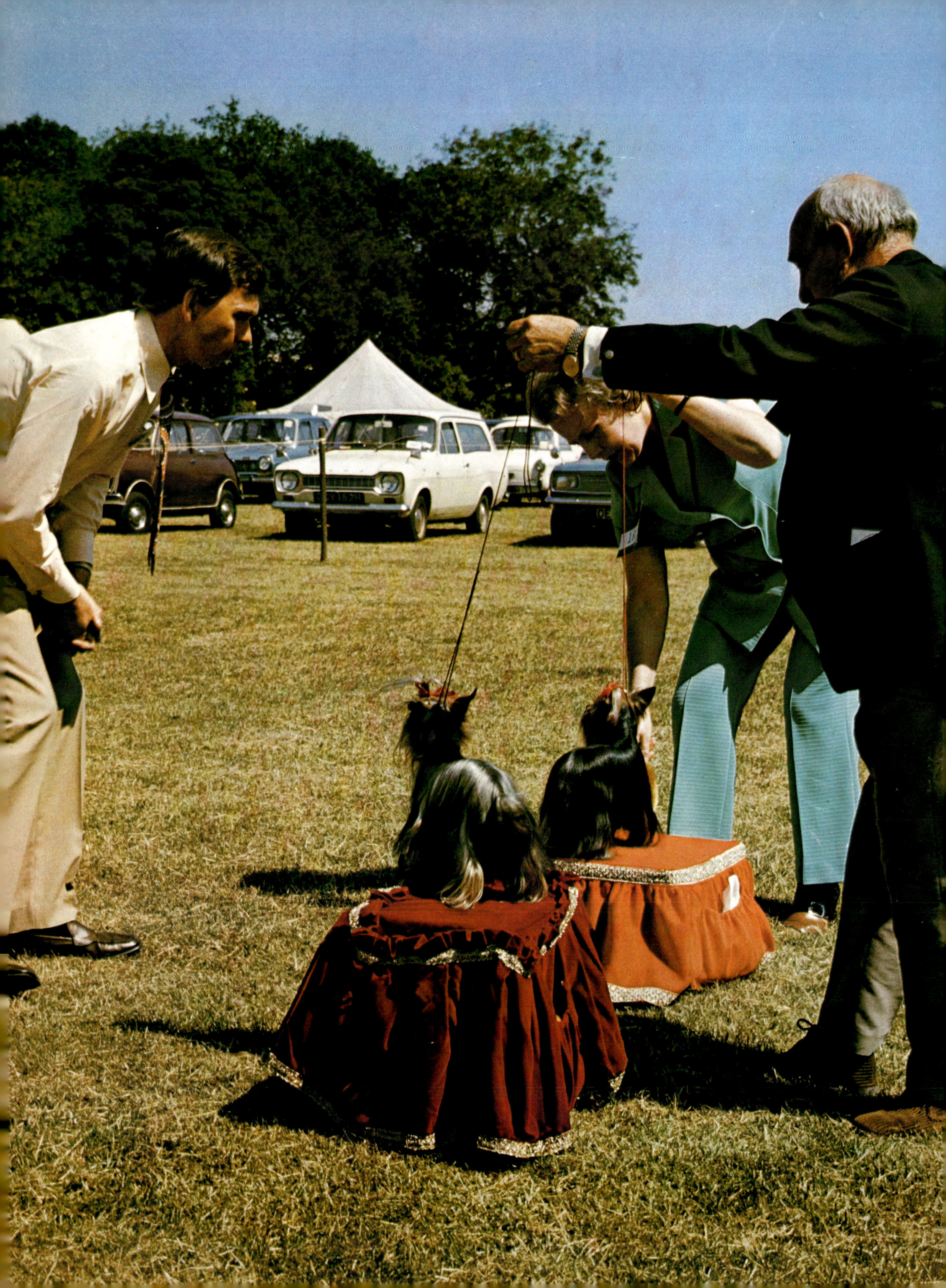

# Dog shows

It is a marked trait of the human race that as soon as two or more people own something or can achieve something unusual someone will want to form a club or prove who has the best collection. As far as showing dogs is concerned we may be quite sure that human competitiveness can only be in the dogs' best interest.

Dog shows, at all levels from the local village array of hounds to top-dog shows, help to maintain standards in pedigree dogs, ensuring that the best animals are used for breeding.

At local level, exhibiting dogs helps to ensure that owners take an active interest in their dogs, grooming them to perfection and keeping them healthy and well. Judges at a dog show not only look for the best shaped dog, the most alert, the most attractive and so on, but they maintain standards of health and vigour.

The earliest shows of dogs were probably held in pits with selected dogs matched against bears, each other or in contests against rats. And although it is true to say that these illegal and disreputable exhibitions in no way are comparable with the respectable and commendable present-day dog shows, they did serve a purpose of enabling dogs which had certain characteristics and attributes to be selected as representative of their breed.

Villany and dogs, especially in towns and cities, seemed to make an abhorrent pair in early times. When the great London fairs of Bartholomew, Greenwich, Southwark and May Fair were in their heyday, bull-and-bear baiting ranked alongside cock fighting, prize fighting and cudgel playing. At these fairs the sporting curriculum was extended to include races for women and fights between women. It was not until 1835 that an Act of Parliament prohibited bear-baiting in England.

As soon as it became unlawful for dogs to be matched against other animals in a vicious manner, most owners turned to more sociable pursuits with their cherished animals – but an atmosphere of competitiveness remained. The first recorded organized dog show in Great Britain was held in Newcastle on Tyne in June, 1859. There were two distinct classes: one for Setters and the other for Pointers. Then, in 1873, the British Kennel Club was formed, which subsequently set standards which were taken up throughout the world.

The interest in showing dogs spread through Europe. In Belgium a show of Pointers was held at Tervueren on 28 May 1847. The first Irish dog show was held in Dublin from 26–31 March 1863.

As the cult of dog showing spread, governing bodies were set up in many countries. Today, anyone thinking of entering a show should contact the organization in his or her country. The standards and rules do vary within breeds from one country to another.

The British Kennel Club, by their introduction of standards, at a stroke made it possible for dog owners throughout Britain to compete at shows and to know what constituted perfection in their particular breed. Furthermore, it enabled dog owners from all over Britain to show their dogs at one central place and to a set standard.

In 1903 the British Kennel Club took the decision to declare what nowadays might be construed as a closed shop. They declared that all dog shows in Great Britain must be held under their rules and regulations. This implied that dogs exhibited at shows not using their rules and regulations would be excluded from shows held by the British Kennel Club.

Needless to say, this at first caused great opposition and discontent, until it was realized that this was the only way to conduct dog shows in a clean and honourable way, to the same standard throughout Britain.

**Types of Dog Show**
The chief requirement for your dog if you wish to enter him for a show is that he must be pure bred. This does not mean to say that if you have a mongrel you will not be able to have the fun and excitement of

Left: When at shows, Yorkshire Terriers are exhibited on gaily decorated travelling boxes. It takes many hours to keep the dog's coat in perfect condition.

Left: Poodles are lively dogs, always full of liveliness and bounce. When shown, they are often in the lion clip. Traditionally, this is said to derive from when the breed was used as a gundog and entered water to retrieve game. The hair was shaved in parts so that it did not impede swimming, but was left on the joints to protect them from the cold. Right: The Lakeland Terrier comes from the Fell country in the north of England. He is an attractive fellow, with a well balanced head and a narrow body. Nowadays, the show dog displays a dense coat, thinned out to give a cleaner and smarter appearance.

entering him in a dog show, for there are plenty of local shows with classes open to him.

Dog shows in Britain are graded from Championship shows through to Exemption Classes at the bottom. The *Championship* is open to all recognized breeds, a Challenge Certificate being awarded to the Best Bitch and Best Dog in each breed.

The *Open Shows* are open to all competitors, but *Limited Shows* are confined to owners who are members of the society or club holding the show. For *Sanction Shows,* again it is necessary to belong to the club or society holding the event. The *Matches* can be exciting events, and they are chiefly held in the winter for members of the club or society holding the match. At the bottom is the *Exemption Show,* where unregistered dogs may be exhibited.

In America all showing and registration is under the rules of the American Kennel Club. The method through which a dog becomes a Champion differs greatly from that used in Britain, and relies mainly on a points system. There are five classes: Puppy, Novice, Bred-by-exhibitor, American Bred, and Open. In addition there are two other classes: Winner's Bitch and Winner's Dog. Under this system a dog becomes a Champion when he has received fifteen points.

In Australia each of the seven states has its own kennel club. However, there is an Australian National Kennel Club which acts in an advisory capacity to these State Clubs. As in America, Champions are selected on a points system.

Showing in most of the Continental countries is conducted to the rules and regulations of the *Fédération Cynologique Internationale,* which is based in Belgium. There tends to be fewer classes than in British shows. The Scandinavian system differs from both the Continental and British shows. Only two classes are scheduled: Junior and Open. Dogs are graded and given a First, Second or Third, or in some cases an o if a certain standard is not achieved.

The golden rule to remember when exhibiting in your country is to obtain a set of rules and regulations from your own national kennel club, and to study them before entering for a show.

**Classes at Shows**
The shows, of course, are graded from the Championships at the top through to the matches. Similarly, each show has classes which are graded, to ensure that everyone stands a chance of winning. It is wise to consult the Show Secretary if you are not sure in which class to enter. Show Secretaries tend to be very aware of the novice and his uncertainty and they make special efforts to ensure that each competitor knows exactly what to do.

There are, of course, show schedules which give information. The Show Secretaries may also be able to give you details of the standards expected from a particular breed. This details the general appearance of the dog, with specific mention to the head and skull, eyes, ears, mouth, neck, forequarters, body, hindquarters, feet, tail, coat and colour, as well as any faults within the breed for which the judges will be specifically looking.

All of this information, of course, varies from breed to breed, and similarly the preparation of each type of dog.

**National Dog Shows**
Shows are held throughout the world and perhaps the main ones staged in English-speaking countries are the Sydney Royal in Australia, Westminster in the USA and Cruft's in Britain.

In each of these famous shows there is a Best in the Show winner, often reflecting the most popular dogs in that country. For instance, the show winners at

Westminster in America during the last ten years have included the English Springer Spaniel twice, in 1971 and 1972, and the Lakeland Terrier twice, in 1968 and 1976. Other breeds to have been the best in the show have been the Skye Terrier (1969), Boxer (1970), Standard Poodle (1973), German Short-haired Pointer (1974), Old English Sheepdog (1975) and Sealyham Terrier (1977).

At the Sydney Royal, during the last ten years, the Afghan Hound has been the best in the show four times, in 1970, 1972, 1975 and 1977. Other breeds have been the Foxhound (1968), Dobermann Pinscher (1969), Samoyed (1971), Australian Terrier (1973), German Shepherd Dog (1974) and Pekingese (1976).

At Cruft's dog show, in the last ten years, the German Shepherd Dog has been top twice, in 1969 and 1971. Breeds to have been top once are the Dalmatian (1968), Pyrenean Mountain Dog (1970), Bull Terrier (1972), Cavalier King Charles Spaniel (1973), Saint Bernard (1974), Wire-haired Fox Terrier (1975), West Highland White Terrier (1976) and English Setter (1977).

## Preparation for the Show

Before you do any showing yourself, take the opportunity to visit a major show and to have a look at the preparation just prior to the dogs being judged.

Much of the preparation, however, goes on throughout the year in the feeding of the animal. An undernourished animal is not likely to win many awards. Indeed, it is better to have a slightly overfed dog with rounded lines, but not one which is fat and flabby.

Regular exercise and grooming is essential. It is no use giving the dog sudden and concentrated grooming for three or four weeks just prior to the show.

Do remember that a spayed bitch may not be shown unless she has first had a litter already registered at The Kennel Club. Also, a dog which has had a vasectomy or been castrated cannot be shown.

*Warmth.* This is a vital factor in producing a dog fit for shows. Some breeds thrive better than others in the cold, and some need warmth to get a perfect bloom on their coat. A sudden spell of cold may send a dog into a moult just when he is to be shown and this is disastrous. Whatever temperature suits your dog try to maintain it.

*Routine feeding.* Dogs like a routine with their food, but if your dog is prone to travel sickness do not feed him prior to the journey. If you arrive at the show without much time to spare and it also happens to be his feeding time, do not give him a meal before going into the show ring. If you do, there is a chance that after a car journey he may be sick, or, more likely, he may fall asleep after the meal.

## Travelling to the Show

This is usually done by motorcar nowadays, and it is prudent to ensure that the dog is well used to car travel. Dogs which have vomited all over themselves can neither look nor smell attractive.

If you decide upon giving the animal a pill to prevent travel sickness, do ensure that he is used to taking it. These pills tend to make the animal go to sleep, and it would be most unfortunate if this happened just before entering the show ring.

Take care not to excite the animal too much and

Left: The Afghan Hound is one of the most attractive and distinctive dogs with a coat of almost any colour. He is a dog specifically bred to chase game, and has the amazing ability of being able to turn very sharply and at the same time not to lose speed. He requires plenty of exercise and grooming. Right: The Chow Chow has been used for many purposes, including pulling small carts, acting as a gundog, and being eaten as a delicacy! He has a characteristic scowling face and a bluish-black tongue.

make him sit still if this is possible. If it has been raining it may be necessary to carry small breeds into the hall, as their feet and under parts can become dirty and wet.

**At the Show**
Handling the dog correctly in the show ring is essential and it is an education to watch an experienced handler at work in the ring. The dog will soon realize if the handler is full of confidence, and if not this will be reflected in the dog.

There are professional handlers who specialize in preparing dogs, physically and mentally, to appear in the show ring. Some of these handlers are very successful in inducing a dog to demonstrate his best points. They endeavour to conceal the animal's faults, if he has any.

Many people engage handlers to show their dogs, and this is far more common in America than in Britain. The owners can then sit back and see their dogs handled to perfection. It would be a pity to detract from a potentially winning dog by careless showing in the show ring.

It is often confusing if at one show the judge gives your dog a high placing, while at another show a very low mark is received. This is most likely to happen because different judges see a dog in different ways. One judge's idea of a certain breed's stance might be totally different from his colleague's. It is nothing more than that – but it is something that the exhibitor has to live with.

If it is cold, put a warm coat on your dog. In most halls, especially in the autumn and winter, there are draughts, so try to keep him out of them.

Some dogs who are accustomed to the routine of shows and have seen it all before get rather blasé and go to sleep. If they do, wake them up at least ten or so minutes before the show and give them a trot around.

A large show hall can be rather frightening to a dog, especially a highly strung one. He may fret if you go away and in this case it is better to have a friend with you who could fetch and carry things for you.

Judges will look at the carriage of your dog, whether he is lively and alert and if he responds to words of command. But liveliness does not extend to allowing your dog to run around sniffing at all the other competitors and becoming a nuisance.

And a point worth making is not to bring a bitch into the show ring when in season. In the early stages of being in season it is possible, by giving her deodorant preparations, to show her. But bitches in season do not generally show themselves very well, and it is a waste of time taking her and being a nuisance to other people.

The dog needs to be trained to stand still while the judge is looking at him. As a nervous and excited dog tends to be snappy it is essential to keep him relaxed and at ease.

## Technical Terms

While at dog shows and talking to the exhibitors you will invariably come across technical terms; some are self explanatory, others need a brief explanation.

*Apple headed.* A dome-shaped skull as distinct from a flat one.

*Apron.* The long hair on the throat and brisket forming a frill. This is chiefly seen on most Spitz dogs.

*Bad shower.* A dog which just cannot display himself

Above: Small dogs like this Yorkshire Terrier are usually judged standing on a table. Right: The hustle and bustle of the Airedale ring at the world-known Crufts Show, which is held in London.

at a show, however good his general condition might be.

*Barrelled.* A dog that has marked rotundity about the chest, often at the expense of depth.

*Beard.* The profuse, rather broad and busy whiskering of the Griffon Bruxellois, as distinct from Terrier whiskers.

*Belton.* The lemon or blue flecked colour of certain English Setters.

*Blaze.* A white mark on the forehead.

*Bloom.* Glossiness or good sheen of the coat, which is desirable in many smooth coated breeds.

*Blue.* Strictly speaking this is a blue grey, as in the Bedlington Terrier.

*Brisket.* The front of the chest, between the forelegs.

*Broken colour.* Where the main colour is broken up by white or other hairs.

*Brush.* The type of tail which has long bushy hair.

*Butterfly nose.* Having mottled skin.

*Button ears.* Those which fold over in front, neatly drooping their tips forward.

*Cat feet.* Compact and round feet, having the knuckles well arched.

*Cheeky.* The pronounced development of the cheeks.
*Cloddy.* A low and very thick-set build.
*Close lying.* A coat in which the body hair lies flat and snug on the body, as in the Labrador Retriever.
*Cobby.* Compact and short in the back.
*Cow hocked.* Having hocks turning inward.
*Cropped.* In some breeds the ears are cropped or cut to various defined erect shapes. This is illegal in Britain and some American States.
*Dewlap.* The loose and pendulous skin under the throat, as with the Bloodhound.
*Down faced.* This is when the nose-tip is well below the level of the stop due to a downward inclination of the nose (opposite of *dish faced*).
*Feathering.* The long fringes of hair as seen on the backs of the legs of Setters and Spaniels.
*Felted.* A coat which has become matted.
*Fly ears.* Semi-erect ears in which the tips are not necessarily carried symmetrically.
*Frog face.* A face in which the nose is extended and the jaw recedes.
*Grizzle.* A term used for an iron grey colour.
*Hare feet.* Feet which are rather long and narrow with the digits well separated.
*Height.* The height of a dog is measured vertically from the ground to the top of the shoulders.

*Hound marked.* When the body patches conform to the conventional pattern of hounds.
*Kink tail.* Any tail with a kink or sharp bend in any direction.
*Kissing spots.* The attractive spots on the cheeks of some toy dogs.
*Layback.* The receding nose in some short-face breeds.
*Lippy.* When the lips are developed or overhang more than is correct.
*Mane.* An abundance of long hair about the top of the neck.
*Merle.* A term for the ancient blue grey mixture flecked or ticked with black.
*Otter tail.* A tail which is much thicker at the root and tapers away, as in some Retrievers.
*Pastern.* The lowest part of the leg, below the knee on the foreleg or below the hock on the hind leg.
*Pile.* The thick undercoat of a medium or long coated dog, as in the Old English Sheepdog.
*Prick ears.* Erect ears, as in the Alsatian and Corgi.
*Rangy.* A rather elongated body and usually loose limbed.
*Ribbed up.* A compact dog with ribs nicely placed.
*Ring tail.* A curled tail which almost completes a circle.
*Ruff.* The frill or apron of long stand-up hair around the neck of some breeds.
*Set-on.* This refers to the part of the hindquarters where the root of the tail is in the body.
*Sickle tail.* A tail which forms a semi-circle.
*Snipey.* A dog is snipey when his muzzle is weak and narrow.
*Splay feet.* Feet which have toes which are spread wide apart, as in some breeds which are used in wildfowl hunting.
*Squirrel tail.* A tail which curves forward over the back, even from the root.
*Sting.* A tail which is fairly thin, even at the root and tapers away to a fine point, as in the Irish Water Spaniel.
*Throaty.* A dog with an excess of loose skin around its throat.
*Trousers.* The hair on the hindquarters of a dog, with special reference to the Afghan Hound.
*Tulip ears.* Ears which are carried erect, slightly open and leaning forward.
*Undercoat.* The soft furry wool beneath the outer coat, which is often of a different colour.
*Wall eyes.* Eyes which are parti-coloured white-and-blue.
*Whip tail.* A tail which is stiff and straight, as in the Pointer.
*Whipcord tail.* A tail which is much too thin for the breed of dog to which it is attached.
*Withers.* The point at which the neck joins the body, about the shoulders.

103

# Index

Page numbers in italics refer to illustrations

Aberdeen Terrier, 75
Affenpinscher, 54, 58
Afghan Hound, 76, 100, *100*, 103
African Lion Hound, 79
African Wild Dog, 7
Aguara–Guaza, 7
Airedale Terrier, 25, 70, *103*
Alsatians, 80, *86*, 103
Australian Cattle Dog, *82*, *83*
Australian Heeler, 82
Australian Silky Terrier, 58
Australian Terrier, 58, *67*, 70, 100

Basenji, 76, *94*
Bassett Hound, 37, 76, *77*
Beagle, 25, 37, *41*, *45*, 76
Bedlington Terrier, *66*, 70, 102
Belgian Barge Dog, 26, 80
Belgian Congo Dog, 76
Belgian Sheepdog, 54
Black-and-Tan Terrier, 53, 54, 74, 75
Bloodhound, 53, 66, 76, 103
Border Collie, *81*
Border Terrier, 70
Borzoi, *26*, 76
Boston Terrier, 37
Bouvier, 82
Boxer, 25, *28*, 80, *86*, 100
Brittany Spaniel, 66
Brussels Griffon, *see* Griffon
Bull Terrier, 59, 70, 100; miniature, 59

Cairn Terrier, *64*, 70, 76, *91*
Cavalier King Charles Spaniel, *52*, 57, 100
Chesapeake Bay Retriever, *68*
Chihuahua, 9, 53, 54, *61*
Chinese Crested Dog, 58, *61*
Chow Chow, *29*, *101*
Clumber Spaniel, 69
Cocker Spaniel, *16*, *36*, 69
Collie, 37, *81*, 82; bearded, *23*, *51*, 82; rough-coated, *20–21*, *42*, 82; smooth-haired, 82
Colpeo, 7
Congo Bush Dog (Basenji), 76
Corgi, 82, *82*, 103

Dachshund, 24, *38*, 62, 76, 82; long-haired, *38*, 78; miniature long-haired, 59; miniature smooth-haired, 59; smooth-haired *38*, 78; wire-haired, *38*, *39*, 78
Dalmatian, *12*, *43*, 100
Dandie Dinmont, 70, 76

Deerhound, *26*, 78
Dingo, 7, 82
Dobermann Pinscher, 57, 80, *88*, 100; miniature Pinscher, 57, 58

Elkhound, 78, *78*
English Bulldog, 75
English Setter, *34*, 65, *69*, 100, 102
English Springer Spaniel, 24, *62*, 69, 100
English Toy Terrier, 54

Field Spaniel, 69
Finnish Spitz, 78
Fox Terrier, *17*, 25, *65*, 74; smooth-haired, 74; wire-haired, 25, *46*, *65*, 74, 100
Foxhound, *50*, 100

Gazelle Hound, 79
German Shepherd Dog, *13*, 80, 100
Golden Retriever, *40*, *44*, *48–9*, 66, *68*, *86*
Gordon Setter, 65
Gray Fox, 7
Great Dane, 80
Greyhound, *18*, 60, 78
Griffon Bruxellois, 54, *55*, 55, 58, 102
guide dogs for blind, 81, *86*
Gypsy Dog, 66

Hounds, *72*, 76–9
Hungarian Pumi, 82
Husky sled dog, *84*, 87

Irish Setter, *34*, 65
Irish Terrier, 74
Irish Water Spaniel, 69, *71*, 103
Irish Wolfhound, 9, *41*, 79, *79*, *92*
Italian Greyhound, *55*, 60

Jack Russell Terrier, *10*, 58–9, *64*
Jackal, 7
Japanese Spaniel, *55*, *59*

Keeshund, 80
Kelpie, 82
Kerry Blue Terrier, 74
King Charles Spaniel, *52*, 55, 57
Komondor, *82*, *83*

Labrador Retriever, 9, *32*, 66, 80, 82, *86*, *92*, 103
Lakeland Terrier, 25, 74, *99*, 100
Large Munsterlander, *95*
Lesser Newfoundland, 66
Lhasa Apso, *22*, 80
Lion Dogs, 53, 57

Maltese, 54, *55*, 57
Manchester Terrier, 54, 74
Maned Dog, 7

Mastiff, 80, 87
Mexican Coyote, 7
Mexican Hairless Dog, 37
Mexican Temple Dog, 54

Newfoundland, 37

Old English Sheepdog, 24, 37, 82, 100, 103
Old English Terrier, 75
Otter Hound, 76
Owtcharka, 82

Papillon, 53, *56*, 57
Pekingese, *27*, 53, 55, 57, *59*, 100
Petit Brabançon, 54
Pointer, 62, 65, 66, *97*, 100, 103
Police dogs, 81
Pomeranian, 57, *58*
Poodles, 25, *53*, 59–60, 88, *98*, 100; miniature, 59
Portuguese Cattle Dog, 82
Pug, 53, *57*, 58
Pyrenean, 37, 100

Raccoon-like Dog, 7
Red Setter, 65
Retriever, 37, 65–6, *68*, 80, 103; curly-coated, 65–6, 70; flat-coated, 66
Rhodesian Lion Dog, 79
Rhodesian Ridgeback, 79
Russian Wolfhound, *26*, 76

Saint Bernard, *41*, *47*, *89*, 100
Saint Hubert, 76
Saluki, 79
Samoyed, 100
Schipperke, 80
Schnauzer, 60; miniature, 60
Scottish Terrier, 75, 76
Sealyham, *46*, 75, 100
Setter, 37, 65, 66, *97*, 103
Shetland, 82
Skye Terrier, 75, 100
Somali Wild Dog, 7
Spaniel, 24, 37, 53, 103
Spitz, *51*, 57, 78, 102
Staffordshire Bull Terrier, 75
Sussex Spaniel, 69

Talbot, 76
Terrier, 62, 66, 70–76
Toy, 25, 53–61, *53*, *55*, *59*
Toy Poodle, *53*, 59
training, 12, 16, 26, 81, 90, 92–5

Water Spaniel, 69, *70*
Waterside Terrier, 70
Weimaraner, 70, *75*
Welsh Corgi, 82
Welsh Springer Spaniel, 69
Welsh Terrier, 25, 75
West Highland White Terrier, 75, 100
Whippet, *71*, 79, *92*
White English Terrier, 75

Wolf, 7
Working Terrier, 70

Yellow Labrador, *87*
Yorkshire Terrier, *56*, 58, *96*, *102*

# ACKNOWLEDGEMENTS

The publishers would like to thank the following organisations and individuals for their kind permission to reproduce the photographs in this book:

Animal Photography end papers 9, 12, 16, 22, 24, 26, 30, 44, 51 above, 53, 54, 55, 59 below, 60, 61 above and below, 64 below, 69, 70, 71 above, 70 above left, 78, 83 above, 88, 91, 92, 93, 94, 99, 100, 101; Bavaria-Varlag 29; Camera Press 18, 68 above; Colour Library International 8, 20–21, 41, 52, 62, 76 above right; Anne Cumbers 17, 23, 32, 36, 64 above, 65, 74, 79, 81, 83 below, 98, 102; John Moss 37, 45, 56 above, 57, 71 below 82, 87; Dick Polak 33; Popperfoto 28; John Rigby 34; Spectrum 14–15, 27, 38, 40, 42, 43, 46, 96; Syndication International 11, 19, 50, 103; Barbara Woodhouse 10; Zefa 39, 84–85 (Deyle) 63, (M. Nissen) 66, (W. Schmidt) 51 below, (Trenkwalder) 47